LUX AETERNA
The Eternal Light

The Mystery of Alchemy and the Quabalah
in Relation to the Mysteries of Time and Space
and The Emerald Tablets of Thoth (Hermes Trismegistus)

**THE LIGHT ETERNAL --
THE MYSTERY OF ALCHEMY AND THE QUABALAH
IN RELATION TO THE MYSTERIES OF TIME AND SPACE
AND THE EMERALD TABLETS OF THOTH (HERMES TRISMEGISTUS)**

by Elias Gewurz
Additional material by Master Occultist Dragonstar
Compiled and Formatted by William Kern
Edited by Timothy Green Beckley
This edition Copyright 2008 by Global Communications/Conspiracy Journal

All rights reserved. No part of these manuscripts may be copied or reproduced by any mechanical or digital methods and no exerpts or quotes may be used in any other book or manuscript without permission in writing by the Publisher, Global Communications/Conspiracy Journal, except by a reviewer who may quote brief passages in a review.

Revised Edition

ISBN   1-60611-009-8
           978-1-60611-009-6

Published by Global Communications/Conspiracy Journal
Box 753 · New Brunswick, NJ 08903

Staff Members
Timothy G. Beckley, Publisher
Carol Ann Rodriguez, Assistant to the Publisher
Sean Casteel, General Associate Editor
Tim R. Swartz, Graphics and Editorial Consultant
William Kern, Editorial and Art Consultant

Sign Up On The Web For Our Free Weekly Newsletter
and Mail Order Version of Conspiracy Journal
and Bizarre Bazaar
www.ConspiracyJournal.com

**Credit Card Order Hot Line: 1-732-602-3407
PayPal: MrUFO8@hotmail.com**

THE HIDDEN TREASURES OF THE ANCIENT QABALAH
BY ELIAS GEWURZ

"And cherish deep within thy heart the memory of those who have served as a channel of light to thy perplexed soul, and be thou grateful to them." —
From the Golden Precepts of Trismegistus.

VOL. I

THE TRANSMUTATION OF PASSION INTO POWER

YOGI PUBLICATION SOCIETY

Masonic Temple
Chicago, Ill.
[1918]

This text is in the public domain in the US because it was published prior to 1923.

The substance of chapters one to six inclusive has been read before the Krotona Lodge of the Theosophical Society during May and June, 1915. Chapter eight was given before the Krotona institute during the session of February-March, 1915. While chapter seven was read before the Krotona Lodge on the 19th of January, 1915.

THE ETERNAL LIGHT AND THE EMERALD TABLETS OF THOTH

WHAT IS THE QABALAH?

The Qabalah is the Secret Doctrine of the Jews, handed down throughout the ages by the great teachers to their beloved disciples under the solemn vow of secrecy.

In the Twelfth Century, however, the principal text-book of the Qabalah was written down by a very learned Rabbi named Moses de Leon. This book is known as the Zohar, and contains inexhaustible mines of occult knowledge. Priceless treasures of mystic lore are scattered in its volumes, awaiting discovery by the intelligent student. The language of the Zohar, however (the Hebrew Chaldaic), known to a very few scholars only, constitutes the main difficulty in the way of those desirous of studying the Qabalah.

The learned assemblies of olden times, in which the great Masters of Israel held forth their doctrines, have been the original sources of the philosophy of these latter days. Modern Occultism, too, is derived from the same quarters, and should the pages of the Holy Qabalah be accessible some day to the English student, he will be astonished and delighted at the wealth of occult truth he will find in them.

The books of the Qabalah are fountains of living waters and at a time of great need, as the present is, the strength and consolation offered us through its teachings are doubly welcome.

The greater part of my life has been devoted to this study, and the teachings given out in my books are all based upon this ancient wisdom of the Rabbis.

ELIAS GEWURZ.
Krotona, Hollywood, Los Angeles, California, May, 1915.

THE ETERNAL LIGHT AND THE EMERALD TABLETS OF THOTH

CONTENTS

Foreword—The Mystical Secrets Of The Qabalah by Dragonstar

Chapter

I. THE VESSEL IN WHICH TRANSMUTATION TAKES PLACE

II. THE FEMININE ELEMENTS IN MAN AND THEIR REDEEMING POWER

III. SPIRITUAL COMPANIONSHIP BETWEEN MAN AND WOMAN

IV. THE KNOWLEDGE OF GOD OBTAINABLE THROUGH LOVE PURE AND UNDEFILED

V. THE MYSTERY OF TIME AND SPACE

VI. THE PEACE THAT PASSETH UNDERSTANDING

VII. JUSTICE AND MERCY

VIII. ON THE THRESHOLD OF THE SANCTUARY

IX. THE ETERNAL LIGHT ACCORDING TO THE QABALAH

X. REGENERATION ACCORDING TO THE QABALAH

THE ETERNAL LIGHT AND THE EMERALD TABLETS OF THOTH

QABALISTIC PRAYER

Rabbi Eleazar, the beloved disciple of the Heavenly flame (Rabbi Simeon), was pondering over the words of the Psalmist, **"And unto the broken in heart the Lord is nigh."**

"Master," he said, "why should it require the breaking of the heart in order to bring God nearer to us?"

"My dear child," replied Rabbi Simeon, "the heart of man is ruled by a multitude of powers; their hold upon it is due to Karmic debts, and every attachment is an obligation of past lives. The ineffable light of the Holy One cannot shine through us until these obligations are discharged. It requires a transparent medium to reflect a flame; dense and opaque bodies do not transmit the light falling on them. It is the shine with the heart of man; when its bonds are broken, God draws nigh unto it."

THE ETERNAL LIGHT AND THE EMERALD TABLETS OF THOTH

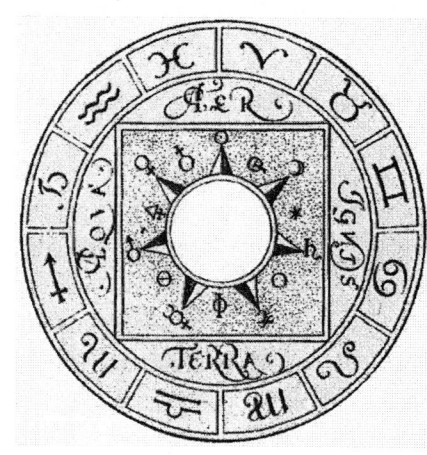

The Mystical Secrets of The Qabalah
By Dragonstar

The Qabalah is not a holy book as are the Vedas, the Bible, and the Koran. It is not a book at all: instead it is a secret traditional knowledge, the hidden thought of Israel, which, like gold embedded in rock, is to be found only after much labor in many Hebrew works, such as the Torah, the Talmud, the Mishna, Midrashim, Zohar, and scores of other books.

This wisdom is formed within a vast number of doctrines, such as the nature of God; the mystical cosmogony of the universe; the destiny of the universe; the creation of man; the immutability of God; the moral government of the universe; the doctrine of good and evil; the nature of the soul, angels, and demons; the transcendental symbolism of numbers and letters; the balancing of complementary forces, etc. All these many problems are divided under two main headings, the Theoretical and the Practical Qabalah; the first being again divided into the Symbolical, Dogmatic, and Speculative branches.

The first main division, that is the Theoretical, is philosophical; the second is magical and is largely elaborated round the Maaseh Merkabah - the Chariot of Ezekiel and the four Animals which are also mentioned in the Apocalypse. Out of this magical Qabalah much of the magic of the Middle Ages was developed.

The universal mystical spirituality of the children of Abraham is a robust, precious, and little known heritage upon which the fabric of the Judaic, Christian, Islamic, and perhaps even the Tantric religions are woven. That heritage is called the Mystical Qabalah, though it is often seen as "Kabbalah" or "Cabala."

Within the context of Rabbinical Judaism, this mystical tradition has come to be known as the Jewish Kabbalah, and in Islam, as Sufism (Arabic

THE ETERNAL LIGHT AND THE EMERALD TABLETS OF THOTH

tasawwuf). The Christian Cabala emerged from the mystical side of Christianity, which developed as a parallel tradition to Pauline dogma as it diverged and became estranged from its Judaic roots. The Christian Cabala evolved as a way to harmonize Jewish kabbalistic doctrines with Christian theology. The precise usage of the word Qabalah to denote the ideas and practices of the esoteric teachings and the secrets of the Torah emerged from the circle of Yitza'aq the Blind (1200 C.E.), and was used in the same context by Eleazar of Worms (beginning of the thirteenth century).

The word Qabalah (lit. receiving, also "welcoming of God") alludes to a dynamic state of direct communication and mystical union of the individual soul with the Divine. In that sense, it is synonymous with the Sanskrit word Yoga (lit. union with or absorption in the Divine). The rich spiritual potential of the Mystical Qabalah has long been hidden and overshadowed by the preponderant visibility of the Magical or Practical Qabalah, whose disciples pursue power as a tool of their own will. The wonderful possibilities for deep spiritual awakening, intensified devotion, and selfless service to the Divine Will offered by the Mystical Qabalah have also been made difficult to access by the strict halachic barriers and confusing intellectual hurdles erected by Rabbinical Jewish Kabbalists.

The life of the early Israelites would have had much in common with all nomadic tribes who dwelled in tents under the starry skies of the desert savannas of Canaan and the Sinai Peninsula. Such tribes were largely extended families who tended their flocks and engaged in the labors necessary to feed and clothe themselves.

It is likely that the religious observances of the Hebrews would have involved quintessential spiritual practices dating from antiquity and found in all monotheistic religions. These practices include: ablution, prostration, invocation of Divine Names, devotional singing, prayer offerings, ritual use of sacraments and sacred regard for the elements, community-building rituals based on the mystical significance of rites of passage and seasons of nature, and the special treatment of guests.

In the Torah, there are numerous accounts of holy figures ascending to and worshipping at power spots on special mountains. There are also several accounts of the ritual use of a stone lingam, over which was poured a libation of oil or perhaps milk. Numerous passages in the Torah also poignantly allude to the experiential transformation of individual consciousness in Divine Union, and the presence and importance of mystics and awakened souls throughout the history of the Hebrews and Jews.

THE ETERNAL LIGHT AND THE EMERALD TABLETS OF THOTH

The monotheism of Master Abraham did not simply mean that there was only one God, but rather that the Divine Source alone exists. Hence, the mystical focus of the early Hebrews would have centered upon the universality and pervasiveness of the Divine Source within all beings on all planes of existence. Group ritual would have underscored and celebrated this relationship.

THE PRIMEVAL ORIGINS OF QABALAH

The origins of the Qabalah are primeval; they are lost in the mists of legend, magic, and folklore. They have grown through a process of mystical integration until they have absorbed all the great myths of the world. The Qabalah is consequently a universal philosophy, combining the eternal masculine and the eternal feminine, and cementing them into the eternally human. So it happens that wherever we search we find origins. Thus in Essenism we find Qabalism.

The Essenes were not to divulge the secret doctrines to anyone...carefully to preserve the books belonging to their sect and the names of the angels or the mysteries connected with the Tetragrammaton and the other names of God and the angels, comprised in the theosophy as well as with the cosmogony which also played so important a part among the Jewish mystics and the Kabbalists. But long before the Essenes existed, there was the Quabalah. Aryan and Chaldean esoteric doctrines percolated into it. In Egypt, the mysteries of the Sun god, the Moon goddess, of Osiris and Isis, impinged upon it. Assyria and Babylon gave it much, and not a little may be traced to the Vedas, the Upanishads, the Bhagavad-Gita, and the Vedantas, and much of the Practical Qabalah to the Tantras more especially.

The Qabalah is traditionally traced back to Adam and Eve. It has been maintained in its purest forms by unbroken lineages of known and mostly unknown masters, saints, and prophets over thousands of years. The practices of the Mystical Qabalah, passed down from teacher to student, generally involve a variety of yogic disciplines that are rooted in scriptural revelations and primary texts. The highest intentions and experiences of the Mystical Qabalah correlate with those of all other mystical traditions. At the same time, and without contradiction, each mystical tradition has its own unique totality archetypes, scriptures, Messiahs and great souls, and styles of observances.

The disciplines of the Mystical Quabalah are distinct from those practiced by magicians, wizards, and sorcerers who seek to acquire creative and/or

THE ETERNAL LIGHT AND THE EMERALD TABLETS OF THOTH

destructive power, depending on what paths they traverse on the Tree of Life. The occult disciplines of wizards and magicians are often called the Practical, Hermetic, or Magical Qabalah. Practical Qabalah has its ancient roots in the "Thirteen Enochian Keys" of Enoch son of Qain, along with a highly eclectic admixture of material taken from Egyptian, Mesopotamian, and other non-Hebrew sources. It is important not to confuse Enoch son of Qain with Enoch son of Yared.

The former Enoch was the grandson of Adam and the son after whom Qain was said to name a city.Torah B'reshith 4:17. Enoch son of Yared was the great, great, great, great grandson of Adam, and the one who "walked with Elohim" and was transformed into Metatron. The ascension and transformation of Enoch ben Yared is vaguely alluded to in Torah B'reshith 5:24, and related in detail in I Enoch, the first of the two remaining books of Enochian literature traced to the reign of Sheba in Ethiopia. I Enoch was translated by R.H. Charles in the late nineteenth century.

In the Qur'an, Metatron is referred to as Al Khidr. The "Thirteen Enochian Keys" of Enoch son of Qain are reflected in such works as The Book of the Sacred Magic of Abramelin the Mage, the Greater and Lesser Keys of Solomon, and medieval grimoires such as the Armadel, Goetia/Lemegeton, etc.S.L. MacGregor Mathers translated The Sacred Magic of Abramelin the Mage, the Greater and Lesser Keys of Solomon, and the Grimoire of Armadel. These books were drawn upon by both the Golden Dawn and Ordo Templis Orientis for some of their rituals and experiments.

Aleister Crowley incorporated material from them in his writings as well. Mathers also brought attention to the Sifra Detzniyutha and the Idra Rabba with his English translation of Knorr Von Rosenroth's Latin translation of those texts. The primary text of the Mystical Qabalah that appears to occupy a central place of importance in the Hermetic Qabalah is the Sefer Yetzirah (Book of Formation).

The two most prominent contemporary schools of Practical or Hermetic Qabalah are the Golden Dawn and the Ordo Templi Orientis (O.T.O.), which still exist and continue to attract followers today. The Golden Dawn was founded in the late nineteenth century in the heyday of the Victorian Period. The document reputed to be at the foundation of the Golden Dawn system was the Cypher Manuscript attributed to Fraulein Sprengel. The Sacred Magic of Abramelin the Mage was also an important document for the Golden Dawn and a significant influence on the controversial Aleister Crowley, who broke with the Golden Dawn and formed the Order Templis Orientis. The

THE ETERNAL LIGHT AND THE EMERALD TABLETS OF THOTH

O.T.O was founded primarily upon works of sexual mysteries and Masonic Charters, and incorporated the Abramelin material at a later date.

THE SOURCE OF MYSTIC POWER

As science is a universal understanding of things, and as the Qabalah purports to be the key to universal wisdom, then, if this wisdom fits this understanding, will this key unlock the door before which we blindly stand. What then is there common between science and the Qabalah?

We know that man is a mystery shrouded in a mystery which we call the universe; and this mystery leads us to a yet deeper mystery which we call God or the Unknowable. All is a three-fold wonder, a relationship between God, man, and the universe.

This universe comes from some unknown source and wends its way towards some unknown end. As it comes from -?, appears to be proceeding towards -?, and is in itself -?, its nature, form, and powers can only be described by means of symbols; that is in pictures which in themselves are no more real than a photograph is real when compared to the thing it represents.

As symbols are but thoughts set forth in pictorial form which possess no activity, we conclude that the world in which we live, and which in fact is shadowed forth by our thoughts, is no more than one infinite thoughtform, a form which exists (how is beyond our understanding) in God, or the Unknowable, and which finds its activity in our thoughts by being fragmented by our finite minds.

To us our thought would be impossible without light, and light would be incomprehensible without darkness, just as heat is incomprehensible without cold. To us, in its ultimate form, the universe is light; it is that which opens the mind of the thinker, which, however, cannot comprehend the existence of light without lack of light.

This light reveals to us a universe of four dimensions, of four worlds in one manifestation, of space and of time the former being built up of three directions, length, breadth, and thickness. The one encloses or includes the other, and what is beyond this four-dimensional universe is unknown, if not unknowable.

In its turn darkness reveals to us the limitations of human knowledge. Our minds may be compared to fire-flies flitting about in the cavern of night. The minute glow which they emit and cast on the void not only shows us how vast is our ignorance, but that all our knowledge can be no more than rela-

THE ETERNAL LIGHT AND THE EMERALD TABLETS OF THOTH

tively true, for the mind is finite and the cavern apparently infinite.

As all knowledge can be no more than relatively true - that is never free from ignorance - wisdom consists in recognizing this fact and of utilizing knowledge in accordance with circumstances. Understand the circumstances and through knowledge extract light (higher Knowledge) from them - this is wisdom; but to use knowledge in order to extract power (the clash between light and darkness) - this is magic.

Wherever we turn we come up against a three-fold order: within man in the form of the physical, moral, and intellectual spheres of his activities between men in that of justice, culture, and work: between man and the universe and between man and God - between everything. Nothing in this world is single; not even a thought is single. All things and all thoughts are relative; that is, they are the offspring of a relationship, of an above and of a below.

Relativity is, consequently, the secret of deliverance from darkness; therefore it is the road towards the expansion of light. And as light grows, so does thought grow. Consequently, when light has reached its utmost limits, thought will do likewise, and the one Thought-Form will be re-created.

This we feel is the ultimate end of the human will - the myriads of fragments of thought reestablished in the Primal Idea. Finally, this transfiguration can only be accomplished through action that is through will to think or to stop thinking. The world we live in is a world of activity, a conflict between light and darkness, knowledge and ignorance, good and evil. It is a whirling energy - nebular force, stellar force, planetary force, human force. It is a world of perpetual revolutions - a cosmos, a chaos, a void, the spark of a new thought; and then once again a cosmos, a chaos, and a void, the shadow of a dead thought.

Nature abhors a vacuum; hence life is the plenitude which fills it, a plenitude which of necessity can never stand still. Each true thought; a thought full of light, which flashes on the darkness which surrounds it, is a Christ unto this world. When three such thoughts, one in the physical realm, one in the moral, and one in the intellectual, simultaneously flash forth, then is a Messianic Age begotten. It is this three-fold deliverance which the world awaits - a deliverance and transfiguration which can only come from within.

THE FOURTH DIMENSION

According to J. F. C. Fuller, author of The Secret Wisdom of the Qabalah, the universal source of mystic power should be given another name in or-

THE ETERNAL LIGHT AND THE EMERALD TABLETS OF THOTH

der to bring it more closely into touch with the ideology of today. Fuller referred to it as the fourth dimension. Here we have no "up" or "down" in the common meaning of these words; for "up" and "down" are attributes of the three-dimensional space in which we consciously live, and to four dimensional consciousness this space and all it contains is nothing more than a mathematical abstraction - a mere notion of the mind.

In spite of the immateriality of the three-dimensional world when viewed from a four-dimensional position, it is possible, as we shall show later on, for a three-dimensional being to establish contact with this source of mystic power, that is to tap it; but once it is tapped it is only possible for the recipient to make use of this power in accordance with his three-dimensional nature. Consequently many of the great religious teachers have insisted on the absolute necessity of their disciples' "purifying" themselves, so that when they attain to the mystic power it may find an equilibrated habitation. For instance, morality, though a gate to the spiritual life, is in no sense its sanctuary; for it is but one of the three great gates - equilibrium of body, heart, and mind.

The reason why such innumerable disputes and persecutions have arisen out of the teachings of so many of the Masters is that they have considered morality, and frequently sexual morality, as the only gate and the only end. Misunderstanding the meaning of moral equilibrium, which demands a balancing of all the moral and so-called immoral forces, and not a suppression of any one category of them, they have so completely contorted the three-dimensional medium that when it receives the mystic power a diabolical state is created. Some have gone so far as to command their followers to neglect and macerate their bodies, and others have asserted that the intellect must be annihilated in order to create a vacuum for the onrush of the spirit. The dreadful consequent is that these errors do not prevent attainment; in fact, in many cases they hasten it by cutting down resistance. But what kind of attainment do they lead to? The vision of X, the Unknown God, on entering a balanced medium or body, becomes the Logos; but when it enters an unbalanced body it becomes the Anti-Logos. True, in both cases the fire brought down from heaven is identically the same fire, but according to the medium it inhabits it illumines or blinds.

Those attracted towards this four-dimensional state are such as …liphas LÈvi calls "the energetic and active spirits", that is individuals possessing strong three-dimensional powers - a deep insight into good and evil, the positive and negative currents of life. As beneath, so above; it consequently

THE ETERNAL LIGHT AND THE EMERALD TABLETS OF THOTH

follows that mundane force is attracted by spiritual force, that the stronger the currents of life the more they are drawn towards the currents of That which created life. And as the mundane force cannot exist without evil, any more than an electrical current can exist without negative electricity, the terrible danger is that spiritual power, like dynamite, can either blast the rock from which the Temple is to be built or blast the Temple which is already built and into which this highest of explosives is off-loaded.

Mystic Power is diabolical as well as divine - according to circumstances. The object of attainment is greater knowledge, understanding, and wisdom of the reality of existence - the Who behind the These. This wisdom in itself cannot assist mankind, though it may utterly change the life of the recipient. It is not the spirituality of the recipient which will tell him how to utilize the power he is charged with, but his intellect, his knowledge, understanding, and wisdom of mankind - that is the mundane shadows of the supernatural realities.

This higher wisdom is a forward impulse of the three-dimensional wisdom, which is a compound of good and evil - the opposite or complementary forces. It is a forward impulse of the will, but with this difference: that whilst in the three-dimensional world a man normally makes use of virtue to enhance virtue and of vice to enhance vice - that is things built upwards - an individual who has experienced the four-dimensional vision, on his re-entering three-dimensional consciousness, sees things upside down. Consequently it happens that, unless his intellect has, as in a telescope, been provided with a lens which will reverse the object, he will affirm with all the frenzy of religious faith that the world is standing upon its head. As he knows (three-dimensionally) that the world should stand on its feet, and as he believes (four-dimensionally) that this reversion is necessary to salvation, he will in actual fact turn the world upside down in order to attain his end.

To him in his higher wisdom virtue and vice are equivalents, for both are illusions when compared to reality; therefore, according to his nature, he desires to establish reality in the three-dimensional world, and if by nature he is vicious he will attempt to transmute good into evil, and, if virtuous, evil into good. In both cases he will be attempting the impossible. Should he, however, have equilibrated the good and evil qualities of his three-dimensional nature before attaining to the vision of the fourth, knowing that all conscious conceptions are illusionary, after attainment he will remain silent and radiate forth spirituality in place of making graven images of its source.

To will, to dare, to know, and to remain silent are the four supreme pow-

THE ETERNAL LIGHT AND THE EMERALD TABLETS OF THOTH

ers of the Magus, and the fourth is the divine synthesis of the preceding three. Those who attain to the fourth (the final letter of the divine name) are the leaders of light - the man Jacob who wrestled with Tetragrammaton at the ford of Jabbok and who did not attempt to pronounce his name. Those who attain to the first three only are like Jason, who cast the cubic Stone of the Wise into the midst of the host of warriors (unbalanced forces), who at once turned upon one another in anarchy.

Not one of the great historical religious Masters was a true Messiah; because no man, however sublime may be his nature, can redeem mankind. There is no short cut to heaven, for mankind will find deliverance only when it creates the power which can deliver it; and when it does so, then spontaneously will the Messianic Age be born. Of all these Masters, probably the most sublime was Gotama Buddha, because he refused to discuss the soul, the nature of God, and the joys of heaven. He said: Think rightly, act rightly, live rightly, and deliverance will be revealed to you. He did not say: "Accept my thoughts, my words, my life, and salvation is yours." He spoke in parables and locked up the mysteries in his heart; for he understood the sublimity of the true Logos-the Unspoken Word.

The most difficult thing with Qabalah is to know what we do know, and what we do not know. Therefore, desiring to know anything, we shall before all else determine what we accept as given, and what as demanding definition and proof; that is, determine what we know already, and what we wish to know. In relation to the knowledge of the world and of ourselves, the conditions would be ideal could we venture to accept nothing as given, and count all as demanding definition and proof. In other words, it would be best to assume that we know nothing, and make this our point of departure.

But unfortunately such conditions are impossible to create. Qabalah and knowledge must start from some foundation, something must be recognized as known; otherwise we shall be obliged always to define one unknown by means of another.

Looking at the matter from another point of view, we shall hesitate to accept as the known things—as the given ones—those in the main completely unknown, only presupposed, and therefore the things sought for. Should we do this, we are likely to fall into such a dilemma as that in which positive philosophy now finds itself—and by positive philosophy I mean a general trend of thought based on the data of those sciences which are now accepted as experimental and positive. This philosophy is founded on the existence of matter (materialism) or energy: that is, of a force, or motion,

THE ETERNAL LIGHT AND THE EMERALD TABLETS OF THOTH

(energeticism); though in reality matter and motion were always the unknown x and y, and were defined by means of one another.

It must be perfectly clear to everyone that it is impossible to accept the thing sought as the given; and impossible to define one unknown by means of another. The result is nothing but the identity of the unknown: x=y, y=x. This identity of the unknown is the ultimate conclusion to which positive philosophy comes. Matter is that in which proceed the changes called motion: and motions are those changes which proceed in matter.

In general, to a disinterested observer, the state of our contemporary science should be of great psychological interest. In all branches of scientific knowledge we are absorbing an enormous number of facts destructive of the harmony of existing systems. And these systems can maintain themselves only by reason of the heroic attempts of scientific men who are trying to close their eyes to a long series of new facts which threatens to submerge everything in an irresistible stream. If in reality we were to collect these system-destroying facts they would be so numerous in every department of knowledge as to exceed those upon which existing systems are founded. The systematization of that which we do not know may yield us more for the true understanding of the world, Qabalah, and the self than the systematization of that which in the opinion of "exact science" we do know.

The Qabalah views all of these separate entities as manifestations of a single force, or as little bits of glass reflecting the one Light. The history of the Qabalah, and of the Qabalists, is a record of those who sought this oneness in a world of diversity.

THE ETERNAL LIGHT AND THE EMERALD TABLETS OF THOTH

The Vessel in which Transmutation Takes Place

Our birth is but a sleep and a forgetting, The soul that rises within our life's star has had elsewhere its setting And cometh from afar Not in entire forgetfulness And not in utter nakedness But trailing clouds of glory do we come from God who is our Home. —Wordsworth.

I.
THE VESSEL IN WHICH TRANSMUTATION TAKES PLACE

Man is fearfully and wonderfully made; he is the meeting point of descending and ascending nature; the arena in which the mighty Gods fight their battles, and principalities and powers strive for mastery over it.

The nature of man is so intricate and complex that even this physical constitution alone has not been exhaustively explored as yet.

There are still chambers within chambers and regions within regions, mysterious and unknown. Now if this is so the physical body, which is plainly visible to our senses and the organs and parts of which can be touched and handled, what about our mental and spiritual natures which are much more subtle and more elusive?

If we lack certainty as regards the body, how great must our ignorance be when we approach the celestial vehicles?

And yet we cannot say we are without knowledge regarding our higher nature, and much has been given to this generation for which preceding ages longed and yearned in vain. Knowledge has been flowing into our minds for the last four or five decades which has dispersed both the superstitions of the Dogmatic Churches and the arrogant Dicta of the official scientists. But knowledge, no matter how plentiful and profound, is no remedy for human ills, unless it is accompanied by love and by the desire to apply it to its proper use. On the contrary, of two ill-disposed persons the one who knows most is

THE ETERNAL LIGHT AND THE EMERALD TABLETS OF THOTH

the more dangerous because as his weapons are sharper, they can do more harm.

And, in fact, it so happened that with the advent of knowledge, its abuse grew apace, and side by side with the good, which it brought into the world, it gave birth to all sorts and conditions of evil.

The great mistake made by the seekers of knowledge, a mistake which proved most fatal to their spiritual welfare, was that they sought knowledge for its own sake. This was bound to result in failure and to frustrate the very object of their search. Man's mission on earth is to attain freedom; lie must be freed from all that binds him to earthly associations. This endeavor is the supreme task of man individually and of humanity collectively. The alchemists of old illustrated this pilgrimage of man towards liberation by their various processes, tinctures, and manipulations. Their vessels, laboratories, metals and transmutations were so many names for the one and the same thing, namely, the illumination of the human soul and her redemption from matter. The well-known saying, "To dissolve and to coagulate" meant nothing but to tear asunder the bonds of passion binding the soul to matter and having dissolved even the most subtle threads of desire and attachment, to turn the life stream upwards and to coagulate it with the pure elements of the Soul. The vessel in which this process takes place is the body of man. This vehicle of manifestation is the crucible in which the pure gold is tried and proven, the alloy and the dross burned away, so that only the sterling substance remains

The human body is the real cross upon which crucifixion takes place. Each Ego chooses its own kind of cross according to its special need. If our body happens to be weak and handicaps us in life's race, it is not a misfortune, a misfortune though it seems.

It may be awkward from a material point of view, but looked at from the higher vistas of the spirit it is invariably a blessing and contains some great lesson of which the Ego is in dire need.

It must therefore be borne in mind that while transmutation takes place, and until it is complete, the vessel, which is the body, must needs suffer from the effects of the process going on within it. If the man has been living a riotous life in the past and then suddenly turns the other way about and wishes to become a saint, he cannot do so in the twinkling of an eye; his various bodies, which as we know are living and knowing organisms, do not at once submit to the change of front on the part of their owner. They feel that they ought to have been consulted about the transaction and they make their griev-

THE ETERNAL LIGHT AND THE EMERALD TABLETS OF THOTH

ances known by various pains and aches and discomforts. These are generally the symptoms accompanying the process of transmutation. The laboratories of Nature are conducted on the same principle everywhere. Whether it is the chemist trying to compound a medicine or the alchemist trying to create a new substance, they both base their practices upon the eternal and invariable law of affinity which governs the generation and growth of every thing in the vast realms of manifest nature. A little reflection will convince us of this perfect analogy subsisting between nature and man and will help us so to order our lives as to profit by all the wise provisions which she has made for the welfare of leer creatures in all the kingdoms.

When man first turns his eyes heavenward, praying to be lifted up, the task confronting him is tremendous indeed. The age-long associations of body, mind and soul have to be severed and new affinities have to be established. Looking at these things from outside we say one must exercise "self-control." I wonder whether any one of us realizes the fullness of the glory of that human being who has really overcome. It really amounts to the making of a new creature, one ceasing to be a man and beginning to be a God.

We understand, of course, that the real battle is going on inside the man. What we see on the surface are only moving hands on the dial of a clock; the clockwork is inside. The springs of conduct are hidden from our eyes; the cause of things is beyond our ken. We often believe we know ourselves and our interests, but the real man and his real needs pass our comprehension. In his infinite wisdom, the Supreme Lord has thus ordained it that self-knowledge should come to man by degrees. While his nature is being transformed, the knowledge of Self filters in. Just look at the four kinds of yoga taught by the Eastern sages. They were designed to facilitate this introduction of Self-knowledge into the mind and the establishment of normal relations between the Divine and astro-mental parts of man. Raja Yoga was to purify the lower man, Karma Yoga was to turn his energies into sacrificial work, Gnani Yoga was to refine his manasic vehicles by mental exercises and study, and at last Bhakti Yoga was to unite him to God by love and devotion. To most of us it is not given to tread all the paths at the same time; we are limited by our congenital failings, and heredity and environment are against us, so as some of us enter the Path we usually progress along the lines of least resistance.

If we are of a practical turn of mind we become Karma Yogis, if students, we become Gnanis, if we are strong-willed we subdue our bodily and psychic natures and become Raja Yogis, and if our natures are affectionate and the love element is the strongest then we become Bhaktis. All of these lead

THE ETERNAL LIGHT AND THE EMERALD TABLETS OF THOTH

to the same goal and at last merge into one another.

He who strives for liberation must finally master all. Yoga like Alchemy requires the whole Man; compromise is out of place in these altitudes, and he, who reserves to himself a little foible or some pet indulgence and thinks it will be all right in spite of all, will find it very expensive indeed, because the ladder will give way and the rung he thought he would skip will prove a pitfall for his feet.

The analogy between Yoga and Alchemy is so perfect and so instructive that one cannot help admiring that wonderful spiritual guidance from on high which leas come down to the founders of both these sciences.

You are aware that Yoga comes from the East, while Alchemy comes from the West. I believe that no great work has ever been accomplished by man on earth without help from those Spirits of just men made perfect, who are always around us like clouds of witnesses to render help wherever needed.

Now the System of Yoga has been taught for centuries in India and the practices of Alchemy have been studied for ages in Europe. Both these schools have had helpers in the higher spheres who inspired their labors. That the teachings of both agree in their essential principles is one more proof of their Divine origin. Now the most salient feature of both Yoga and Alchemy is their agreement as to the vessel in which the operation is to take place. It is the body of man; by body I do not mean the physical vehicle only, but the mental body as well. Both have to be put in the furnace and purged from their old dross until the glorified spirit is free. "To produce gold one must have gold" is a Hermetic saying; well, the gold is the spiritual soul within us. It is she who has to be resurrected from the ashes of Self sense and sin so that she may enter into her rightful possessions of the Divine Gifts of virtue, wisdom, and love promised to her by the Giver of all good gifts, the Father of Lights from whom she comes. "Life itself," says Patanjali, "is the great teacher of Yoga." The cosmic procession of life passing before our eyes is the High School par excellence in which the children of men graduate into Yogis of various degrees and rank. Every cycle pushes humanity a little further upon the high road of evolution, and as one spiral is passed and another reached, Man finds he has grown almost imperceptibly in all the graces and accomplishments incidental to the latest stage of unfoldment.

Those who wish to go ahead of their brethren must not wait for the generality of men; they must step out of the beaten track and—as it were—take a hand in their own making. The present moment is very favorable for this independent departure, because the cyclic law favors it and the new dis-

THE ETERNAL LIGHT AND THE EMERALD TABLETS OF THOTH

pensation into which we are entering makes it easier of accomplishment. In the mineral, vegetable, and animal kingdoms, the units undergoing evolution are helplessly subject to the law governing the group-soul; on the human plane only does independent initiative come in.

Arrived at this stage the Jiva-Atma or the Spiritual Soul is at liberty to break loose from the mass and to start on its way back to the source of its origin. This way of return is through the chamber of ordeals, the crucible in which transmutation takes place. All metals must be purified and transformed into gold, which means that all outgoing tendencies must he mastered, drawn in, and turned upward so that they may serve to energize the pure Spirit—and help to manifest him according to his dictates instead of drawing him as hitherto after their own inclinations.

It is impossible to describe the process in particular as, owing to Karmic bonds, we all have different burdens to bear, but on the whole it is safe to say that at any time in our life we are to be found in just that place and surrounded by just those conditions which, if understood and respected, would invariably help us to fulfill the law and by so doing draw nearer to the goal, namely, the liberation of our souls from the bondage of illusion. But unfortunately we are never quite reconciled to the hard facts of this world and this life, and even the best of us think we are in the wrong place and if it were not for this, that, and the other, we might be better off, and have a better chance to be happy and good. But my dear Brothers and Sisters, it is not so!

We are, as I said, at every moment of our lives, just where we ought to be, and happy the man who can realize this truth in all its wonderful simplicity. The vessel of transmutation into which we have been thrown will never give us up until we are quite ready and well done; let us not oppose the process and thus retard the advent of our freedom.

As you are aware, everything in this world is governed by analogy The law that governs the atom is the same which governs man, and the law that presides over the evolution of man is identical with the law that rules the universe. Bearing this in mind, how significant every act of ours becomes! Often even slight and seemingly unimportant actions of ours may, in their ramifications, generate karmic results of tremendous importance to our fellow-men and to the world.

Especially is this true of people of high spiritual status. They are doubly responsible for their thoughts, words, and deeds, because they create corresponding effects upon the higher planes.

"To him to whom much is given, of him much shall be required"; that is to

THE ETERNAL LIGHT AND THE EMERALD TABLETS OF THOTH

say, the man of power must be alive to it, that with the acquisition of power he increases his obligations, and the more powerful he grows, the more sacrificing must he be. When the lower elements of our constitution become transmuted and refined, we acquire great powers and many gifts, and the danger arises that we may not adequately appreciate the solemn duties attaching to them. The law of God can never be broken; it is we who break ourselves in violating its eternal decrees.

Having overcome most desires, as we finally do, in the process of transmutation, we must also overcome the greatest of and most subtle of all desires, and that is the desire for power. Power for its own sake is not worth having, and more than that, it often throws the disciple far deeper down into the abyss than bodily self-indulgence. It is the same with spiritual pride—Pride is the sin against the Holy Ghost, which can never be forgiven. Therefore, when undergoing the transformation of our natures in the crucible of life, we ought to see to it that these subtle and poisonous elements are got rid of in the process.

Let us now recapitulate the main points: As soon as man begins to be dissatisfied with his old life and his old habits and learns to appreciate the grave beauties of the higher life, the process of transmutation is started within his constitution. He may not yet actually have done anything to begin the new life, but the mere resolution to do so plants his feet upon the path. Even to see only the futility of the vain, sinful and empty life, means half the battle won. When a definite step is taken and the desires truly renounced, the Karmic effects are mighty and far-reaching. If the aspirant is strong enough to persist in spite of the trials springing up on every side, as he advances on the Path, then the work of transmutation enters the second stage, which is the stage of unification. Before this is reached, all passion, whether physical or mental, must be rooted out of his nature. Unification is the crown of the great work; it is the reward of ages of effort and aeons of hard labor. Truly blessed is the man in whom the Divine Self has been united permanently to the astro-mental part which is all we see of one another while on earth. When this conjunction has taken place, man has ceased to be subject to the laws of man; for him, we have been told, "no law can be framed"; he has ceased to be a child of earth, for he has become in the truest and deepest sense, a child of God.

Now there is one thought I would like to impress strongly upon our minds at this point. It is this: while this higher and nobler life is eminently desirable and all of us would fain attain unto it, we must not forget the grim reality

of this every day existence of ours arid, while reaching out for the higher life, let us not by some careless act or acts wreck this prosaic foundation upon which the poetical structure of the life beautiful is to be raised.

Many have made this mistake and destroyed themselves body, mind, and estate, in order to develop spiritually. What they really did achieve was entire ruin both physical and spiritual. Let us in our endeavor to live the higher life be as practical as we are in the management of our mundane affairs. Above all, let us be guided by reason and let us discard everything that is cloudy and vague, and after having done all we possibly can do to guard against the blind forces of the lower nature and to master all that is beneath us, let us remember that we are infinitesimal expressions of the one great law, and we can do nothing better than commend ourselves to its Supreme Author, the great Law-giver. He knows us better than we know ourselves and He loves us better too.

And therefore we say unto this last, "Into Thy hands do we commit our Spirit and our souls into Thy keeping."

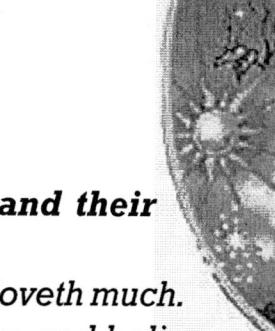

THE ETERNAL LIGHT AND THE EMERALD TABLETS OF THOTH

The Feminine Elements in Man and their Redeeming Power
Much shall be forgiven unto her who loveth much.
Love on, through doubt and darkness, and believe
There is no thing which love may not achieve. —E.W.W.

II.
THE FEMININE ELEMENTS IN MAN AND THEIR REDEEMING POWER

Strength and beauty are the two attractive elements of our nature, but the masculine strength and the feminine beauty are in reality one and the same thing. That which we admire as strength in the man is the same element that fascinates us as beauty in the woman.

The difference consists in the way of their manifestation only. When the spirit has gained sufficient power on the outgoing path and is strong enough to hold the power that is his in eternal potentiality, then beauty appears on the scene and transforms the forcefulness of the man into the gentle attractiveness of the woman.

To be quite exact, beauty is strength on a higher spiral; when strength ripens, it becomes beauty. This is the spiritual aspect of it, that seems to have been voiced by all the sages of antiquity.

Even savage man of prehistoric times was subject to the attractions of the physically much weaker female, thereby acknowledging her superiority over his brute force.

The law which governs the generation of energy on the inner planes of being also presides over the evolution of beautiful forms; the source whence strength springs is identical with the origin of all that is pleasing to our sight.

Man is by nature the aggressor, the moving factor, whose energy makes the plasticity of the world-soul yield her latent treasures.

THE ETERNAL LIGHT AND THE EMERALD TABLETS OF THOTH

Woman, on the other hand, contains these treasures. She is identical with the World-Soul, and in her the strength of man becomes transformed into beauty, which is the higher aspect of strength. Right here I must remind you that in every man is concealed the womanly element just as every woman has masculine qualities. In fact there are such things as womanly men and manly women. Here we are concerned with the spiritual nature, and as regards this, it is well for us to bear in mind that the feminine nature is far superior to the masculine both in its sensitivity to the unseen, and in its capacity of sacrifice and devotion to the ideal.

I do not wish to be understood as depreciating "the mere man." I could not very well do that, but what I want to emphasize is this, that true greatness and nobility of soul are due to those qualities within us which are feminine by nature.

It matters not whether the physical body one wears is that of a male or a female; It is the perfection of the spiritual nature that counts.

Before man can be redeemed his nature must become feminine. Man stands for positive action, while woman is the symbol of passivity. The idea of power is generally associated with active energy, but it requires a stronger will to refrain from action that to act. Therefore is woman's sphere above that of man, and her kingdom must come before man realizes his true nature.

The dissecting and analytical function of the mind is of a masculine character, while the synthesis, the gathering up and consummating, is altogether womanly. This applies to all the realms of nature; to everything under the sun. In the battle of life, while making his pilgrimage through this wilderness of earthly existence, man is like a strong oak, or a trusty, sturdy oaken stem, but woman like a vine clinging in grace and beauty to him.

This expression of female tenderness on the physical plane is only an emblem of the true relation on the plane of spirit. There the companionship is free from the vicissitudes of earth, and partakes of the Divine nature only. The relations between the sexes on the higher planes are in accordance with the heavenly law governing those planes. Those whose good fortune it was to know the pure friendship of a woman on the earth plane have had, even in this life, a foretaste of the Heavenly condition. Its effect upon the physical nature is the same as when the sun draws up the muddy water of a stagnant pool by the roadside, and, changing its vibrations, returns it as the gentle life-giving rain, softening the dry earth.

Thus is the effect of the sweetness and light emanating from a pure soul in

THE ETERNAL LIGHT AND THE EMERALD TABLETS OF THOTH

whom passion has been stilled and desire transmuted.

It is through this recognition of the spiritual elements within us which are of a feminine nature that the atoms, molecules and particles of the physical body become glorified and healed and the mind becomes illuminated.

The human soul is in possession of the greatest of all Divine gifts—the power to heal other souls; mark you—not only bodies, but Souls.

The gift of healing is in itself a great boon to mankind, but, when to it is added the power to heal the heavy-laden soul of man then the possessor thereof is indeed a favored mortal whom the Gods delight to honor. This spiritual gift of healing can only be exercised by that man or by that woman in whom the mind has been dualized, that is to say, it has become male-female in one. In those in whom this process of mind-dualization has been effected, a new life springs up which, compared to the old one, is like light unto darkness. It is here, right here that the redeeming power of the feminine elements in man is seen. At the first birth man is endowed with the earthly mind, but at the second birth he receives the heavenly one. To the twice-born sons and daughters of God all things are possible.

To some of us this exalted state may seem a dream, but dreams and longings are founded upon true being for no one can long for that which has no existence or the possibility of existence. Perception of coming things is only possible through conception. The physical life we live and all the desires of the flesh that appertain to it are like the sacred lotus of Oriental lands. The root of this lotus is buried in mud and slime, but from this lowly condition it rises through the currents of the river until at last it reaches the air. Here the plant blossoms forth in luxuriant purity, a type and symbol of the highest spiritual development.

Thus it is with sex life. Sex life has its roots in the mud of material life; it rises through the flowing waters of mentality and finally blossoms in the clear air of our spiritual nature, pure, sacred, divine.

Those whose feet have climbed the rugged steeps of the spiritual heights and who have at last reached the summit will understand the need of their trials, and the wisdom which ordained them. It is at the very top of the mountain that the spiritual consciousness opens and man becomes aware of his dual nature. Then, when this highest part of his constitution is mature, he can draw unto himself from surrounding nature that which corresponds to this highest and most potent part in himself.

If he has the Gold (Love) within him, he can draw the very highest from the vast expanse of space by virtue of the law of affinity which makes like

THE ETERNAL LIGHT AND THE EMERALD TABLETS OF THOTH

attract like.

There is a fundamental difference between the atomic elements of the masculine and principles in nature and this causes the difference in the external form of male and female.

It is a peculiarity of atoms well known to chemists that their behavior depends upon their arrangement, though their nature is not changed. Thus the difference in the constitution between a molecule of ozone and a molecule of oxygen is quite imperceptible, but their properties differ widely. Why this should be so is a mystery which is perfectly unfathomable to physical science. The key to this mystery is to be found elsewhere; it lies in the spiritual forces governing nature from within. The power that determines the mode of life and activity of an atom, or a molecule, is beyond the reach of the microscope and the scalpel; it is a spiritual power which acts in accordance with laws not yet known to the scientific world. These laws are as beneficent as they are wise, and they invariably make for human well-being. Now if we ascend the scale of creation and examine the workings of these atomic arrangements on the higher planes we find the same law holds good and that duality of sex and its effects upon the life of the human species is just as much a mystery as it is on the lower planes. You often hear of the new mental type which is emerging from the present one; this new type is to be a dualized mind. The holy Qabalah teaches that every thought and emotion is represented structurally in invisible substance, the highest and purest aspirations and emotions consist atomically of bisexual human beings dualized in their mental nature and patterned after the shape of primal man. These forces, however, can only operate through those mortals who are struggling to regain their lost condition of pristine purity by long preparations, severe moral discipline and self-denial. Those who have given themselves to the service of humanity, consecrating their life, thought and substance to the furtherance of God's Kingdom and the doing of God's will on earth, will find that all their old passions and desires, having once been transmuted, will now spring up as powers for good within them. Eliphas Levi, the great Qabalist, left his testimony to this effect. The strength of his devotion to the light he had keen, he assured his pupils, was in exact ratio to the strength of his former passions, a force of which he had by severe discipline subdued and turned into a servant of the God within.

All desire is centrifugal, outgoing, while will, pure spiritual will, is centripetal and attractive. Thus do the feminine qualities in our constitution exercise a redeeming power over our old Adamic nature, and, until man un-

THE ETERNAL LIGHT AND THE EMERALD TABLETS OF THOTH

derstands this bi-une arrangement of his internal make-up, and, understanding it, strives to awaken and deepen the Divine Consciousness within himself so as to become continually and increasingly aware of his duality, there is little chance of his transcending the level of ordinary humanity. But, when this miracle has happened and the eyes of the soul have been opened and the torch of faith has been lit, then man becomes more than man; he has established his right to be a ruler of man.

Christ, the everlasting symbol of all that is true and good and really great, was of a feminine nature. He only wore the body of a man, but His soul was womanly. His life, His labors, His final sacrifice were just the means to fill the measure before His departure from the valley of tears, in which He was to learn all lessons and to suffer all manner of pain, in order that He might be able to help those whose lot in life it was to suffer and to endure. If we wish to benefit by the redeeming power of the feminine elements within us, let us recall the memory of the Lord of Compassion and the agonies of His spiritual crucifixion. It is an ordeal we all must pass through, sooner or later. Let it be sooner.

The supreme message of this ordeal to us is that we may not try to escape from our Karma, but whatever betide us, we should say: "Let this cup pass from me, yet not my will, but thine be done." Thus shall we learn to be patient under tribulation and strong in the day of trial.

Millions of human beings, our brothers and sisters, are waiting for our help. We cannot help them until we have ourselves overcome. The physician must first heal himself if he is to be of any use to the patient. It is a hard path to tread, the path of overcoming; it has been called the path of woe, but it is also the path of glory. When we some day arrive at the end of it, we shall understand the words of the Conquering Christ ringing down through the ages—"It is finished"—"*Consumatum est,*" as the Latin Bible has it. Yes, then, we too shall say "It is finished"; we have fulfilled the cycle of our destiny. Whenever this comes to pass, our sole concern in this life and the things of this life will only be so far as they relate to the spirit's welfare. Henceforth all our striving, if we strive at all, will be, that, as the days pass by, we may grow juster and fairer and purer, more kind and more true, more silent and more humble, and having attained ourselves, to point out the way to the younger souls corning after us. It is the only means we have to repay the blessed Masters for Their sacrifices, which alone have made our lives worth living.

THE ETERNAL LIGHT AND THE EMERALD TABLETS OF THOTH

THE HOLY SUPPER
The Holy Supper is kept, indeed, Whenever we share another's need. Not what we give, but what we share, The gift without the giver is bare. He who giveth Himself with his gift, feedeth three, Himself, his needy neighbor, and Me.

Spiritual Companionship Between Man and Woman
What matter if I stand alone? I wait with joy the coming years; My heart shall reap where it has sown, And garner up its fruit of tears. The stars come nightly to the sky; The tidal wave unto the sea; Nor time nor space nor deep nor High Can keep my own away from me. —Burroughs.

III.
SPIRITUAL COMPANIONSHIP BETWEEN MAN AND WOMAN

In the ancient temples of Egypt and Chaldea they used to tell the neophyte that whenever he met some truly congenial companion during his subsequent career, it would he a sign that the time of his probation was nearing to the end and that he was soon to be recognized and accepted as a disciple of a great Master. As a rule, those who enter upon the path must dwell alone; solitude and loneliness are their lot. It is only when they have learned to stand alone and to remain unshaken that they are allowed the companionship of a friend. The social life of a man distracts the soul and makes it depend upon the whirl and change of events for its sustenance. When the soul is to awaken to its new and true life, these kaleidoscopic changes must give way to constancy and unity. This cannot be the case until man has been tried and proven in the furnace of affliction. When he has tasted of the bitterness of life's cup and emptied it to the very dregs, when one after the other of what we call life's joys have been taken from him and

THE ETERNAL LIGHT AND THE EMERALD TABLETS OF THOTH

he has lost his health, his possessions and his friends too, then a sense of utter loneliness comes upon him and he enters what the mystics call the great void. Here he has to stand his trial. If he passes it successfully, he is admitted into the inner court of the temple, and permitted to know the true character of his Karma and the laws under which it operates.

Ordinarily the children of men are ignorant of Karmic law, and they do not know the ways and the means by which they are judged. But the disciple does know these things and this knowledge enables him to work with the law consciously and intelligently. As soon as he can do that, Karma relaxes its rigidity and, instead of the measure of judgment, the Lords of Karma grant him the measure of mercy. That is to say, he can now partake of the things of this world and be in it, without being of it.

Spiritual companionship is one of the blessings that come into the disciple's life at this period. He begins to recover his friends, but this time they are friends of the soul and hound unto him by ties of spiritual affinity. What a comfort and a joy to the suffering soul when she finds a sister soul here on earth in whose company she can make her pilgrimage to the other shore! Blessed are the souls that do find one another while on their journey homeward bound. The help they can render each other covers many planes; the various forces human beings are possessed of, magnetic, electric, sympathetic, mental, psychic and moral are all capable of being raised to higher planes of activity. They are all biological in their essence, and, as such subject to the dominance of the spiritual will.

The union of two beings strengthens the dominion of the will, and especially is this the case if the union is between members of the opposite sex. The reason for this is the difference in the magnetisms of the male and female bodies. Every atom in our constitution is surrounded by a magnetic circle. This magnetic circle consists of positive and negative particles, balancing each other. The mental and spiritual particles of our higher bodies are likewise constituted. Between two human beings of the opposite sex—provided their mentalities are congenial—the same relation exists on a larger scale. The electric elements preponderating in the male organism are balanced by the magnetic currents of the female body acid the harmonious exchange of the magnetisms thus generated is the cause of that feeling of exhilaration and joy which a pure companionship between man and woman invariably produces. So much so, that it often seems that the physical bodies have no weight, but appear to float along without effort. No wonder that the participants in such a union looked forward with great delight to the

THE ETERNAL LIGHT AND THE EMERALD TABLETS OF THOTH

time when they would meet. The old-fashioned conception of life, the prudery and restraint in the social intercourse of men and women, were responsible for a great deal of harm. Untold misery was the result of most of the marriage-relationships, because the partners did not know each other sufficiently. But apart from it, the most innocent contact between the sexes was looked upon askance by people whose minds have not been pure enough to think of love as a Divine gift that can be expressed on many planes much higher than the physical. Happily, these notions are gradually passing away and man and woman can sustain friendly relations to each other. The evil-minded person, who thinks of wrong at the sight of what is God's most perfect gift to the children of men, that person condemns himself because the evil he sees is in his own mind only. "To the pure all things are pure." To return to our subject, the magnetisms streaming out from the auras of man and woman are differently constituted. Through their interblending, positive and negative life-elements are obtained. This interblending creates life, and life is not a material substance, but a spiritual element, highly refined and potential with great possibilities and with great power.

Now all these benefits to be derived from the association between man and woman are non-existent for those who have not yet mastered their passions and lower emotions. People who live on the lower planes of life may derive a certain pleasure according to their evolutionary status, but this is not what we are here concerned with. The aspirant striving to enter the temple of knowledge and wishing to taste of the heavenly joys of pure and undefiled love must have subdued his desire nature; his mind must be like a limpid lake, calm and tranquil, on the surface of which not a ripple is to be seen.

Having accomplished this purification, man and woman are fit to be spiritual companions, but not otherwise. That it is worth while to go through this ordeal has been testified to by all who have attained unto the goal. There is a love which few have known. It is the love that opens the soul's inner portals and admits our spirit into the holy of holies, the sanctuary of the pure soul. There the glory of the Divine image is restored, and nature crowns the victor with the laurels of a consummate happiness, of which in ordinary life there is naught to serve us as an illustration.

Wisdom, the ultimate aim of life, can only be acquired if the law leas been fulfilled. The fulfillment of the law implies that we have had our share of all experiences—if some of them are missed our education is incomplete. Before we attain unto final liberation we must ascend the ladder of earthly life

THE ETERNAL LIGHT AND THE EMERALD TABLETS OF THOTH

and view from every rung of it the world around us. It is this which is meant when we are told "to look intelligently into the heart of men." We must learn our own lessons, even the highest, by passing through the full gamut of the things which human life has to offer. There are, , two ways of passing it—the lawful one and the lawless one.

The lawful way of gaining experience on earth is the partaking of all it has to offer under the guidance of the Spirit and only in proportion to the Spirit's actual needs. Lawlessness steps in when we desire for the sake of desire and do not respect the Soul's protestations. The disciple to whom desire is only a means of gaining knowledge uses it in accordance with the eternal design which called it forth. On whatever plane desire exists, it is only a means to an end for him and he does not allow it to tarnish his higher nature, or to create within him the germ of attachment to any form or shape of it. This resignation in the midst of the objects of desire is productive of great and lasting strength. The continual balancing of the centrifugal and centripetal forces of spirit generates the Divine power of overcoming all the ailments of body and soul and endows us with the supreme virtue of healing all manner of disease.

The spiritual companionship between man and woman has the acquisition of this power for its purpose. Owing to her experience in past lives, woman's interior nature is more centered in love than man's and consequently she supplies the necessary welding power to hold man's psychical and spiritual natures to a given centre. The Divine self though ever present in both sexes cannot appear to us, unless the love and power elements are blended and eternal silence has been borne in the soul.

As man and woman grow in spiritual worth, their power and influence for good go on increasing and they become focal points for the hosts of heaven watching over humanity. Under the guidance of these guardians, and, while doing their bidding and cultivating their higher nature, man and woman grow in all excellence.

Those treading the path of discipleship find great help in such a congenial companionship. The continuous transmutation of bodily structure is attained and furthered through such soul communion; and through the mental activity consequent upon it, the body is changed cell by cell. This transmutation is the same as the alchemic process by which food and drink and breath are changed into blood, from blood into aerial fluid and then into etheric or mental substance. Then the ego touches it by its own vibrations and it becomes more etherealized into soul or auraic essence.

THE ETERNAL LIGHT AND THE EMERALD TABLETS OF THOTH

Every conscious effort we make to uplift and refine the physical body is a step towards the quickening of our spiritual faculties, the deepening of our insight and the increase in wisdom and understanding. The process of life is a continuous chain of sublimation and refinement.

Beginning with the lowest and crudest forms of matter right up to the highest expression of life, everything is undergoing evolution and transformation. Speaking of matter, we are thinking of tangible material such as we can see or touch or recognize by the physical senses, but air is matter and we live completely immersed in it and in other airs, that is to say, finer elements than the one we call air. In these tenuous regions our evolution is going on while we are unaware of it. But all the same is the substance of those planes subject to the universal law of transmutation. We are, as it were, unconscious agents of nature on those planes, and she uses us to effect her designs everywhere.

The higher virtues of love and devotion subserve this purpose of refinement on the higher planes. You often heard it stated by our great teachers that the sentiment of love purifies the emotional body; so does the sentiment of devotion. It virtually then comes to it that, even when we think that we are acting in a most spontaneous way, bestowing our love upon the object of our affection, or offering our devotion to our ideal, even then we are only instruments of nature who works through us like a clever craftsman in the execution of his plans.

At the same time, we must bear in mind that when we are used as agents on those higher planes, it is well with us because we are then free from the lower forms of Karma to which those on the material plane of life are still subject. This is one of the benefits of spiritual companionship; it advances us by planting within us the seeds of love and veneration and turning the emotional and passional forces of our nature towards the inmost and the highest, thus giving us a foretaste of the pure and selfless Divine love which we shall some day realize on the higher ranges of cosmic life.

To conclude, let us review the main benefits derivable from the association of man and woman in a pure spiritual companionship. First, the relation must be established between people of congenial natures; they must love the same things and be devoted to the same ideal; the more such ideals they have in common, the better for them, for their ties are strengthened thereby.

Second in importance, but not to be underestimated, is the physical constitution of those associating. Some people think they can slight this aspect

THE ETERNAL LIGHT AND THE EMERALD TABLETS OF THOTH

but it is not so. Though true sympathy is of an interior nature, it must not be forgotten that our senses are avenues to the spirit and things that are to commend themselves to the Spirit must be pleasing and acceptable to its sentinels outside, which we call our senses.

Perfect sympathy can only subsist between partners whose bodily constitutions only introduce true harmony into their relationship. Where the slightest repulsion exists, owing to external antipathy, the bond of union must needs be weakened. If harmony has been established on the physical, mental and spiritual planes, and the purpose of the given association is to serve the highest which both partners cognize, then Divine revelation comes to them and enlightens them in all things. It is the Voice of God in the garden telling how to crown the sanctified life with beauty and joy and how to make it a milestone for the wayfarers of succeeding generations.

Star to star vibrates light, why not soul to soul? If the purpose of life is beneficent, as we know it is, is it not the duty of each being to serve as a channel for the spread of light and the increase of joy? When two human beings are united for this object on earth, the angelic hosts on high bless their union and take them into their charge. They are led through the highways and byways of life and shown the untold misery and suffering calling for aid and comfort. Looking round them, they learn how to love those who know not what love is, how to pity, how to help and how to grow God-like. Thus strengthened by their own devotion to each other, they pass along on their mission of mercy, pouring out their benedictions upon the needy and distressed with whom their Karma brings them in contact. Their own pure personal love has taught them love Divine which is purer still.

Having profited by their association in body, mind and soul, they now work on the plane of spirit, as servants of the most high God. Truly blessed is the portion of such, for they have found favor above all other mortals, and, even when all things of earth shall pass away, their loving deeds will live. For such there is no fear of death, for, having fulfilled the cycle of their destiny on earth, they will continue their labors of love in the regions beyond, in the gracious presence of the Lord of Hosts, of whom we are told that "His mercies endure forever and his compassions never fail."

THE ETERNAL LIGHT AND THE EMERALD TABLETS OF THOTH

The Knowledge of God Obtainable Through Love Pure and Undefiled

A picket frozen on his duty, A mother starved for her brood, Socrates drinking the Hemlock, And Jesus on the Rood. And the millions who, humble and nameless, The narrow pathway of duty have trod; Some call it consecration, While others call it God.

IV.
THE KNOWLEDGE OF GOD OBTAINABLE THROUGH LOVE PURE AND UNDEFILED

The vague notions still prevailing among leaders of thought as to what constitutes the summum bonum, the highest happiness, are responsible for most of the chaos of our social life and our systems of education. As long as we are not quite certain as to what the goal of humanity really is, we cannot possibly order our lives to the best advantage. Man's chief glory is the faculty whereby he knows. As long as material conditions constrain him to spend the greater part of his life in manual labor, he cannot of course devote much time to the cultivation of his intellect; but, since the advent of scientific devices for labor-saving, humanity has been in a better position to care for the intellectual upliftment of the masses. The Higher Education has been increasing, art and literature are flourishing and every one, no matter how humble he be, seems to be anxious for knowledge and eager for culture. With the progress of the sciences, however, the problem arose how to utilize their application so that it might result in the greatest happiness for the greatest number. This is indeed a mighty problem, worthy of the attention of the best and bravest of men. How can we use these God-given gifts of inventors and their discoveries, so that they may not result in multiplying human misery but rather in its reduction and final elimination? The answer has not yet been found so far as practical life is concerned. We still use our best energies and

THE ETERNAL LIGHT AND THE EMERALD TABLETS OF THOTH

the most clever intellects to manufacture implements of war and to organize bodies of men against one another. Our economical conditions too are in a state of perpetual disorder. Each man is for himself; millions are perishing annually for lack of the very necessaries of life, and few of us seem to care. There is plenty of food and an abundance of everything to make life comfortable, but the good will seems to be lacking to make all these good things subserve their proper purpose, namely, the welfare of all.

As man masters nature and frees himself from her tyranny, the need for utilizing all her forces to increase the sum total of human happiness dawns upon him. He realizes the vanity of all things which narrow his horizon and the poverty of even the greatest of pleasures if they serve only the petty self. In this age and generation, the waves of social sympathy rise very high and, amidst the indifference of the rich and mighty ones, many a man says to himself, "I am my brother's keeper; his troubles are mine, and I am responsible for his wellbeing." The public institutions we possess, all the social arrangements for the welfare of the poor and helpless ones, who have fallen by the wayside, are due to the efforts of those chosen ones who have realized the seriousness of life, and, wishing to make the best of it, are devoting their possessions and their energies to ameliorate the conditions of the oppressed and downtrodden ones so as to bring a little of the sweetness and light of civilization into the aching hearts of the eternally disinherited. But man does not live by bread alone, and his need of spiritual and intellectual sustenance is just as great and as pressing as that of physical nourishment. The strongest desire of man is to know. He wants to know the world in which he lives, the body he calls his own, the soul he believes inspires him and the God from whom she comes. All these things man wants to know, and the more time advances towards the end of the cycle, the greater grows his eagerness for that knowledge.

After securing the comforts of life and ease and leisure, man hungers for mental and spiritual satisfaction. Of all the defects of the present organization of society and of the cruelties consequent upon it, none is so fatal to the welfare of man as the denial of knowledge to the enquiring mind and of the chance of culture to the aspiring soul. The absence of these opportunities is the most blighting factor of the competitive system, because it deprives man of his natural and legitimate right to acquire all the knowledge he can about himself and his environment. The greatest privileges of man being his capacity to know, anything that denies to him the exercise of this faculty is an unmitigated evil. But it is not only knowledge of material things which the

THE ETERNAL LIGHT AND THE EMERALD TABLETS OF THOTH

mind craves; the desire to know comprehends things unseen as well. The soul of man yearns for nothing more deeply than for the knowledge of God. The vistas of knowledge are infinite, but not even the highest can satisfy the heart of man. It is only in the knowledge of God that man can find lasting peace. "It is possible to know God," says an occult writer, but it is not easy to acquire that knowledge. The Rosicrucians used to say, "In order to know God one must be God," which means that we must transcend ourselves altogether, and reach out to the sublime heights of the Eternal. Unknown to the indifferent and slothful, God reveals himself to the searching heart and rewards its persistent labors and earnest seeking by the supreme gift of the knowledge of Himself.

"To know God is life eternal," says the apostle; the two are identical. For in ordinary life our perspective is limited to this mundane plane, and we can only know by means of the lower mind, but, when our intuition takes the place of reason, and illumination that of speculation, we know, even as we are known.

Here is a Heavenly promise to man: "Those who seek me, shall find me, if they seek me with all their heart and all their soul." The trend of modern life is towards the spiritual side of things. Science and philosophy are both engaged in paving the way to a more intimate acquaintance with things spiritual. Man as a unit, and as a member of the collective body of the human race, seeks for God in everything he does, but he does not always seek Him rightly, which is the reason of his partial success; but the tendency of human endeavor is growing more and more towards the spiritual. In all departments of life men begin to realize the need for a readjustment of values and for the subordination of the material side of life to the ideal one. This leads to numerous improvements in the methods of labor and to social reconstruction.

The love of God, being the crown of the inner life, is thus expressed in practical life in the service of man. That passion, which formerly made for acquisition, is now under the influence of growing knowledge transmuted into the passion for doing good.

Ambition having fulfilled its purpose in former cycles, when infant humanity wanted it as a spur to exertion and action, is now stepping into the background and her place is taken by man's desire to serve and to be useful. "God's own synonym is use," says a wise proverb, and, as we were made in the image and likeness of God, it behooves us, also, to be of use; only thus do we grow Godlike.

THE ETERNAL LIGHT AND THE EMERALD TABLETS OF THOTH

The knowledge of God is best acquired by the practical expression of the Divine attributes in actual life. It is the loving service we render wherever it is called for, which endows us with these attributes. Love, pure and undefiled, expressed in practical every-day life is God's own activity performed by His deputies in human form on earth.

There are two paths of union with God, according to the mystics of old; the path of Knowledge and the path of Love. Those who unite themselves to God by knowledge will sooner or later see the need of love to strengthen the bond of union, while those whose lives are full of devotion must supplement their endeavors by searching and seeking after the deeper mysteries of God-hood revealed by knowledge. The ancient Sages, the great Masters of the Inner Wisdom, taught that the knowledge of God, when obtained, makes of mortal man an immortal. The pure love which helped the acquisition of that knowledge while the disciple was treading the Path, provides him with his glorious garments when he arrives at his destination. These garments are woven of good deeds done, and of noble causes helped during the earthly life; on the heavenly planes their memory becomes the germinating seed for deeds of mercy to be done in future lives. The path of beauty and joy, the path of peace and bliss, converge at the same point. From all sides do the wanderers arrive, but the object of their pilgrimage is the same. It is the temple of wisdom from whence light streameth out in all directions. Humanity has to battle through the iron age with all the horrors incidental to it, before man attains unto his spiritual consciousness. While the battle lasts, every effort counts and every single step taken by the individual pioneers brings mankind nearer to the portals of the sanctuary in which all mysteries will be solved and all tears will be dried. There man will learn to understand the secret of his voyage through the cycles of time, and the purpose of his sojourn on earth. Until that time arrives all our work is only preparatory.

To utilize the fleeting moments, to obey the Spirits' guidance, to detach ourselves from all that drags us down and to join forces with all that lifts us upward, that is our task for the present. The knowledge of God is obtainable and will be ours, but the only way we can attain unto it is by the constant practice of charity in thought, word and deed, and by the expression of love pure and undefiled.

THE ETERNAL LIGHT AND THE EMERALD TABLETS OF THOTH

The Mystery of Time and Space

O, sometimes comes to soul and sense The feeling which is evidence That very near about us lies The realm of Spirit mysteries.—Whittier.

V.
THE MYSTERY OF TIME AND SPACE

Time and space are the fundamental conceptions which form the warp and woof of our thought. We cannot think of anything except it is, was or is to be, and yet, in their very essence, time and space are the most elusive of problems and can never be grasped by the mind of man. What is time? What is space? What existed before time began, and what will remain when time is no more? What does space mean? Is it a homogenous substance of one kind? or is it heterogeneous and formed of a variety of elements? Where does space cease to be? What is there where space is not? Now these are a few questions very interesting indeed and pregnant with thought. We may not succeed in finding a final solution to the lot of them, but we may perchance succeed in contributing a mite towards a better understanding of them.

Science, the interpreter of the laws of nature and of the principles underlying them, cannot help us in our search to solve the mystery of time and space. The proper domain of Science is the physical universe.

This modern archangel (science) has no wings. An invincible giant, when her feet touch the earth, her marvelous power, her initiative, wisdom and penetrating intelligence are all gone the moment she rises above the soil, and, though it be only a few inches, upon this battlefield she is overcome at once—faint and almost inanimate in an unequal battle because she could not readjust her energies to new conditions. At present science is a child of earth and waits for her redeemer, through whom she will be born again a

THE ETERNAL LIGHT AND THE EMERALD TABLETS OF THOTH

child from heaven.

In the matter of positive investigations, science has no equal; she is almost infallible, but she is at once rendered powerless when confronted by a problem of the spiritual order, or even when it concerns a—so to say—mixed problem (such as the genesis of matter or the abnormal organic growths of animals or plants) science is silent, or perhaps just stammers.

Now that which the seemingly almighty scientific mind cannot accomplish by its own unaided efforts, the spiritually awakened soul can, and often does, accomplish. Time and space do not exist for the soul of man. The mystery which they constitute to the earthly mind is non-existent to the enlightened spirit. Time, or the succession of events pertain to things material. On the spiritual planes we live in feeling and thought, and it is the feebleness or strength of these which determines the quality of our life on those planes, and distinguishes one being from another. Space again is equally illusory to the soul. Spirit is not separated from spirit by distance, but by discord of nature, and on the other hand spirit is not united to spirit except by the affinity subsisting between them. We can be thousands of miles away from our loved ones but we do not get estranged from them thereby, whereas we may be very close in space to one wishing us ill, and the fact of spatial proximity will not bring our souls nearer to each other. The eternity of time and the infinity of space can be viewed and grasped by those beings only whose minds have learned to function beyond those concepts. Just like the law of Karma which must be transcended in order to be understood, so must the limits of time and space be got rid of by the spiritualization of our thought before we can grasp their meaning. To incarnate humanity, dependent in a thousand different ways upon material conditions, time and space are necessary conceptions; without them there would be chaos in our minds. But for the liberated soul, even on the earth plane, time and space can be relegated to the limbo of things superfluous.

When man once makes up his mind to live the higher life and to think of every experience as related to the spirit and either helpful or hurtful to it, then time and space will matter little to him. His motive and his action and the spirit that prompts them are all that he cares for, from the moment of his surrender.

The dignity and meaning of our lives do not depend upon the years we have lived, nor does the height of our spiritual stature hear any relation to our physical dimension in space. It is only the things which make for growth in perfection that really do count.

THE ETERNAL LIGHT AND THE EMERALD TABLETS OF THOTH

And, on the other hand, only those events injure us which weaken our faith and obscure the larger hope. The education and spiritualization of our will being the immediate object of our terrestial existence, time and space signify to us only as much as they serve that object. The only other purpose which time and space serve is the lessening of the evils inherent in the lower life of the race.

The evils from which humanity suffers are not eternal, but confined io the limits of time. They diminish and their intensity decreases in the same proportion as humanity expands its life both in space and in time. The end of all those evils will be their ultimate disappearance by being reduced to what geometry call the "infinitely little." It will happen in the same way—to use a simple illustration—as would be the case if a pound of salt were thrown into a bucketful of water; it would strongly salt it, while, if it were thrown into a cistern, it would only very slightly do so. In a pond, its taste would hardly be noticeable, and absolutely nothing would remain of its effect if it were thrown into a river. Humanity's evils, too, will disappear in the infinity of space and the eternity of time.

Time and space are the remedies which can cure the evils afflicting mankind. These evils would be incurable had Adam (the universal man, or group soul) preserved its life unchangeably. He had to be divided in space, in order to be healed and for the sake of his reduction and division ad infinitum by means of time; whenever this division is accomplished time will come to an end, and divisible space will disappear. Then will Adam (the universal life) return to its primitive state of an indivisible and immortal unity.

Death is only a phenomenal change, and of no more consequence to man than the other changes he has to undergo in the course of his evolution. It simply transmutes the human being from the state of visible nature into that of formless and invisible substance, just like birth manifests what was formerly in a state of substance, on the plans of visible nature.

The old Kabbalists used to express it in a like manner: "There is no birth, nor death, only continual change and transformation from state to state. This makes up the being and existence of all the kingdoms, mineral, vegetable, animal and human."

So time and space fulfill their mission by curing the evils from which mankind must needs suffer in its early stages of evolution and by providing the race with the means of redemption from all that is base and unworthy.

Having freed himself from the limitations of time and space, man realizes that he is a citizen of this grand cosmos and that his rights and privileges, as

THE ETERNAL LIGHT AND THE EMERALD TABLETS OF THOTH

an immortal and eternally progressive being, cannot be gainsaid. In the infinity of the universe man feels for the first time at home. He never again fears spiritual extinction, for his deathless soul ensures for him life everlasting. If man identifies himself with nature, he has to be transformed by her, if, with the Spirit, he is redeemed by God.

There is no death anywhere, except the unconsciousness of God's presence. To acquire an abiding consciousness of God's presence means to have transcended both time and space, to live in the spirit and to prepare one's self for service in the higher worlds and vaster systems, where there is neither time nor space, but where the Divine Spirit grows in all excellence and perfection.

To the world at large these things sound strange, but to the children of light, whose affections are set on things above, a glimpse comes now and then of the glories awaiting the man who has overcome.

The process of overcoming is an individual one and can only be known by the soul that experiences it. The words of the prophet remain forever true, "and to him that overcometh I will give to eat of the hidden Mannah, and a white stone will I give him, and on it shall be written a new name which no one knoweth save him who receiveth it."

THE ETERNAL LIGHT AND THE EMERALD TABLETS OF THOTH

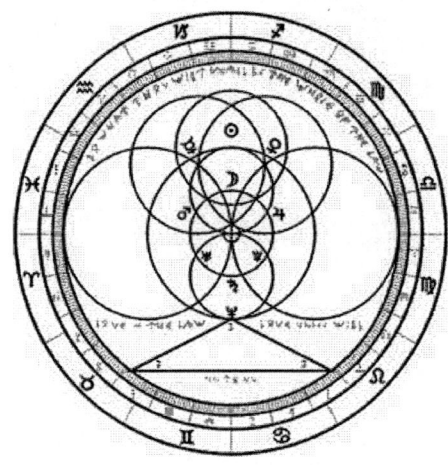

The Peace That Passeth Understanding

For only they who in full completeness Have drained life's wine to its very lees, With all its bitterness and all its sweetness Can joy completely in God's great peace. —Hawthorne.

VI.
THE PEACE THAT PASSETH UNDERSTANDING

Saint was one of those few Church Fathers gifted with the true vision. One of his beautiful sayings is to the effect that "Our hearts shall ever be restless until they find rest in God." In the course of out journey through life we try to assuage our pain by many things. We plunge into work and think that will make us forget the dreariness of our existence, but, failing to find satisfaction in work, we try pleasure, and naturally that, too, is disappointing—even more so. And so again we try mental culture, but with no greater success, and then we despair and begin to wonder whether there are such things as peace and contentment to be found in this valley of tears we call earth. Despair is generally a forerunner of better things, and when a man is good enough to despair of himself, it shows there is still something left in him worth tribulation. This something begins to show its vitality when it alone, of all things, has been left. Tolstoy says that man's worth to the community where he lives and to the world in general, dates from the day on which he knows himself to be worthless—when he loses all, he gains all. To the seekers of peace something similar happens. Peace is a plant which grows in the desert of our inner nature only. When everything has become like a desert, when everything has been dried up, even our tears, when we can no longer cry, and the very flower of life has faded, then Peace germinates in the parched soil of the desolate heart; and, just like the fair flowers in the garden, our lives begin to emanate their sweetest fragrance when we are bruised and

THE ETERNAL LIGHT AND THE EMERALD TABLETS OF THOTH

wilted and altogether trodden down. This applies to the occult life especially; the occult life—the one we have to live in this world, surrounded by its hardships and cares. Our every relation to people and environment is indicative of our occult status. The circumstances are our teachers and, if we do not learn from them, our life has been lived in vain.

Just look at the rose, and its form and color, the fine lovely texture of its petals and its sweet aroma. It is only because the sweet spirit that animates it knew how to adapt itself to its environment and to attract all that was needful for its growth and perfection, that the rose became what it is. The same law holds good on the human plane. Let us be like the spirit of the rose and we, too, shall dispense the benediction of our qualities to all that pass by. Those who seek peace must vibrate it themselves. But peace cannot be found before its time, for it must be borne in mind that for long periods during our evolution strife and stress are necessary. When, however, the time arrives for the soul of man to rest from her toils, there enters the heart a kind of rhythm which we call peace.

Peace is to the heart what rhythm is to matter; even in the physical organism, a kind of rhythmic peace must obtain. The soul's atoms are mingled with other lower atoms, but never combined. An illustration from chemistry will help us to understand this clearly:

Oxygen in pure air is mixed, but not combined, with nitrogen. When these two gases are combined, according to their proportions, the result is a deadly poison. This is exactly the internal process. When the atoms of the various parts are mingled harmoniously, the result is physical and spiritual well-being; when discord ruptures the rhythm of their vibrations and their harmonious balance, disintegration sets in and disease results.

If matter moves rhythmically, it is pleasing to our eyes, and our feeling on beholding it is a restful one. In the heart of man peace fulfills the same functions. Without it nothing of worth can be accomplished by man; while to the peaceful soul all things are possible.

The mistake modern intellectualism makes is in believing that the brain is the real agent in all important work; the serious observer of life knows this to be a fallacy. The brain is not the important part of the house in which man resides. The centre of life is the heart, and, if consciousness does not take its residence in the centre of life, it will become separate from life and cease to be. Those who desire to develop spiritually must think with their hearts.

Man is a constellation of powers in which all kinds of seeds are contained. The heart is the seat of the central power from which all the others derive

THE ETERNAL LIGHT AND THE EMERALD TABLETS OF THOTH

their vitality and inspiration. That they may live and function properly, the central power must be at peace with itself and with each one of them. When this is the case, peace reigns supreme and registers itself in the countenance by an attractive angelic radiance. Kindliness and peacefulness always produce beauty and give the face a touch of heaven, for beauty is the light of the soul reflected in the forms of matter.

All of us have at one time or another met people who were a perpetual mystery to us, owing to their constant and changeless calm. Nothing seemed to ruffle them; they took everything just as it happened, and everybody just as he was. They seemed to desire no change and no variation of anything. They were the people who have discovered the secret of peace. As long as "man's inhumanity to man makes countless millions mourn," that peace is beyond attainment for the majority of the race. When the Sun of righteousness arises some day and man realizes the unity of all that lives and breathes, peace will be his. At present it must be won by a prayer of the individual soul, who feels sorely in need of it. There are thousands of such souls everywhere, and to them the message from on High has come down, "Call upon me and I will answer thee, and I will show thee great and mighty things, and I will heal thee and give thee an abundance of truth and peace."

True prayer has a scientific basis; its effect is as certain as that of any other cause in nature. Let us pray for peace and we shall obtain it, even in the midst of stress and storm. When it enters our hearts, we shall know it by the feeling of reconciliation with which it will suffuse our whole being. After that we shall rebel against nothing. For God is enough, and his abiding presence in the soul of man makes her desire naught else.

Thus in the silence which follows the storm the precious jewel is found. At last the harassed soul is at rest and, self-contained, wishes for nothing outside herself. She has found the peace of God, the peace which the world cannot give, neither can it take it away; the peace which passeth all understanding.

THE ETERNAL LIGHT AND THE EMERALD TABLETS OF THOTH

Justice and Mercy
And enter not into judgment with us,
for in thy sight no living man shall be justified.

VII.
JUSTICE AND MERCY

When does one become a Master? When one has learned all the lessons that earth has to teach. How does one learn all these lessons? By submitting to all the experiences natural to this sphere without repulsion when they are painful and without attachment when they seem to be pleasant. Thus, taking things as they are, and letting them all deliver their message, the period of schooling is shortened for the disciple, and his entrance upon the higher stages of the path begins earlier than would have been the case, had he allowed the various qualities of his constitution, called Gunas in the East, to play havoc with his desire nature or to otherwise detain him. There is a saying, "When the disciple is ready, the Master is ready also." When the disciple is ready means that he has arrived at a stage when he can listen to that voice which has bee&. called "the Voice of the Silence," because: we only hear it when we have passed through the silence and accustomed ourselves to live and move and have our being in it.

The first four rules of Light on the Path show us how to pass through the Silence safely. The rule we shall consider tonight is the third. "Before the voice can speak in the presence of the Master it must have lost the power to wound." There is a little story of an old Rabbi, a great teacher of the Qabalah, whose first few words when arising in the morning were, "Heavenly Father, may I during this day and until I again close my eyes in sleep not be made the instrument of judgment against any brother or sister of mine." At first sight it seems as if this is just a common prayer for help from outside, but it is

THE ETERNAL LIGHT AND THE EMERALD TABLETS OF THOTH

not. Its scientific foundation is the same as the one underlying the precepts in the hall of learning which, as you know, are all truths founded in Nature. In our earlier days, when we used to pray in the old-fashioned manner. the object of our prayers appeared to be to make us good, but later on when we learned to know the true inwardness of things and the purpose of human life, we found that many a thing which sounded as a religious threat was, in reality, a statement of fact inherent in the nature of things. Now, when the Master Hilarion caused to be written down this rule, that "before we can speak in the presence of the Great Ones our voices must lose their power to wound," he did not mean to give us a good bit of advice, with a promise attached to it—that if we are good the Masters will listen to us. No more did the old Rabbi mean anything of this sort. The idea both had in mind is the everlasting truth written in the very heart of the cosmic law. That law determines that on every plane units shall be used for the improvement of their species. We see this law governing the mineral, vegetable and animal kingdoms, but it generally escapes our attention that it also holds good in the human kingdom. Nature in her vast domains uses individuals and entities to further the growth of the collective bodies of which they are the units. Continual progress is nature's aim, and, on the human plane, she achieves it by making every man his brother's keeper. The feeling of repulsion which we experience at a wrong or careless act of a fellow-man is Nature's safeguard against the recurrence of a similar act. She put us where we are in order to eliminate the possibilities of wrong-doing. But now, there are various ways and means of achieving that end. Punishment is one way and instruction is another. On the lower mental level, reaction is so quick and violent that it punishes both the wrong-doer and him who is the witness of wrong-doing, but, on the higher mental level and on the planes beyond it, where the spiritual consciousness is wide-awake, reaction is of a reflective and deliberate character and can select the mode of its response to any form of discordant action. This principle was known to the sages and teachers of the past, but the cycle of evolution did not admit of its universal application. In this century, however, we find it percolating slowly the social conscience, so that even in state-prisons it is found to be better policy to make the confinement of prisoners remedial, rather than vindictive. Now, we as students of the Wisdom-Religion, realize that there must be an exact correspondence of these happenings on the outer plane, within the interior regions of our collective soul life, of which our social structure is but a temporary and transient expression. We see Nature using us individuals as instruments to carry

THE ETERNAL LIGHT AND THE EMERALD TABLETS OF THOTH

out her behests and while so doing refining both instrument and materials. On the plane on which those we call Masters work, there is no room for violence or for anything like it. Correction there is, by means of loving instruction only. Now, as the Theosophical Society is, so to say, the training-ground for future disciples, those who watch over it find it necessary from time to time to communicate to us some of the rules governing life on those exalted planes. "Light on the Path" is such a communication, and the rule we are now considering is the one destined to regulate the relations between individuals aspiring to follow in the footsteps of those Holy Teachers who have learned all their lessons in past aeons of evolution.

Now, apart from the reaction to wrong, which takes actual form by punishment, there is a finer and subtler mode of reaction known as criticism or judgment. To have lost the power to wound, our capacity to criticise and judge must have undergone the same change as the social custom of punishing crime is gradually undergoing. Our very way of looking at things must change. To students of Theosophy this should be easier than to those ignorant of the Ancient Wisdom. We, who know that the personal life is an illusion and that this whole existence is simply Maya, created by Nature in order to evolve the true self, should not find it hard to see that the tendency to wound, whether it be by thought, or word, or deed, is one of the deceptions practiced upon us by external nature, prior to the awakening of our true selves. It is she who makes us resent wrong and repel the wrongdoer. Our True Self knows no resentment and is free from repulsion. In days to come it will be as uncommon to criticise a spiritual failing as it is today to criticise a physical one. Even at the present time, well-brought-up children would not laugh at a blind man, or at a lame one, nor would they make fun of the deaf and dumb; and yet, does it ever occur to us that, whatever the misbehavior, crime or vice of a fellowman may be, if it awakens in us any other feeling than love and pity it is because we are not yet well-brought-up children on the plane of spirit. When the Sixth Root Race arrives there will probably be hospitals for criminals and nursing homes for vicious people, and they will all be treated with the same loving care as we now treat those who are sick in body. It is to prepare us for this stage that "Light on the Path" has been given to us. "Before the voice can speak in the presence of the Masters it must have lost the power to wound." To realize this rule in its fulness means to be free from the tyranny of Nature, and, instead of being unconscious instruments in her hands to chastise and to give pain, we become teachers and helpers and healers, and exercise mercy instead of judgment.

THE ETERNAL LIGHT AND THE EMERALD TABLETS OF THOTH

Every time we are called upon to act, we are faced by our trial, and it depends upon our attitude whether the doors to further progress shall be opened to us.

The first of the vestures we have to lay down at the entrance to the temple is that innate tendency to judge and to criticise, because it is a loveless proclivity of the old Adam, and within the temple there is no room for that which is loveless. Therefore the great Masters of the Inner Wisdom warned us that before our voice can be raised in their presence it must have lost the power to wound. As long as it wounds, man cannot teach, neither can he help. Those who wish to become helpers of the race must not be instruments of judgment, and that is why the old Rabbi, the teacher of the Kabala, prayed every morning immediately after rising, "Heavenly Father, may I during this day and until I again close my eyes in sleep, not be made the instrument of judgment against any brother or sister of mine."

THE ETERNAL LIGHT AND THE EMERALD TABLETS OF THOTH

On the Threshold of the Sanctuary
I know not where his islands lift Their fronded palms in air, I only know I cannot drift Beyond his love and care. —Whittier.

VIII.
ON THE THRESHOLD OF THE SANCTUARY

"Before the soul can stand in the presence of the Master she must have been washed in the blood of the heart." The blood of the heart is, as we know, the life-essence and for the soul to have been washed therein means that life and all that belongs to it of joy and sorrow has been relegated to a secondary place and that the foremost consideration of that soul is now the will of her Lord who has been revealed to her in the process of surrender. It is during this process of bathing in the life-essence that the soul discovers some one, whom alone she would like to serve. During the years of our indiscretion, while we are driven hither and thither by our various likes and dislikes, we serve many Masters, who often prove veritable tyrants to us, but when we have had enough of them, we find that there is a Master of a different stamp, who lives not by our passions and desires, but rather by their suppression and subdual. Now before the soul has made this discovery, it is of no use for her to aspire to the true Masters' presence. In fact, it may harm her to venture thus far. We often find among seekers after truth, persons who have overstrained themselves in one way or another and made themselves physical and mental wrecks in their effort to find and live the higher life. The reason for this is their disregard of the advice given to occultists by all the great and good ones in respect to the dangers of the razor-edged path. You remember how H. P. B., in the "Voice of Silence," admonishes us to see to it that the ladder does not give way while we ascend its rungs.

THE ETERNAL LIGHT AND THE EMERALD TABLETS OF THOTH

The rungs of the ladder on which we climb upward are our weaknesses and bodily failings. To overcome these is our first task before we enter the outer court of the temple. To enter into the Holy of Holies with the old desires clinging to us, spells disaster. No truly-great teacher will accept a pupil who does not seek, by renunciation and by devotion to prove himself worthy of the wisdom which he is striving to attain. In the Gita we are told that no one is to be taught the higher truths who does not practice Tapas, which means renunciation of all that is of the earth earthy. In the too, great stress is laid upon self-control, and the great Yogis of the East have at all times been ascetics first and disciples afterwards.

To stand in the presence of the Master implies to he a channel to their sublime teachings, but how can one serve as a channel who has not been purified? You would not think of drinking water that runs through an unclean pipe, for fear of its having been contaminated. No more can one benefit by a spiritual channel which is not thoroughly clean, for fear of the impurities that may have found their way into it during the process of transmission.

The blood of the heart symbolizes the passions of the earthly man, and, in their control and final extinction, lies the secret of regeneration. The Path of Discipleship is strewn with many wrecks on account of the failure to heed the warnings of our ancient teachers who told us of the many pitfalls on the way. The Master Hilarion, who inspired The Light of the Path and who occupies a high rank in the great Hierarchy, had probably unique opportunities to study the ways and means that best secure and shorten the passage to the other shore. From his exalted position, he could observe those who succeeded and those who failed and he also saw the reason why. In this gem of occult literature, called Light of the Path, he gives us the benefit of his experiences. If we value our higher life we should not neglect so expert an advice as that of Master Hilarion. That which troubles us most in treading the Path is our habit of compromise. We are not whole-hearted and generally do things by halves, the result being that, whenever we enter upon the higher stages of advancement, we find many things to be undone and many a habit to be broken.

In those high altitudes the lightest discord creates wrong vibrations which baffle the young soul just emerging from the Egyptian darkness and not only bar her way to further progress but often throw her back into the abyss of repeated incarnations in matter. This is not a figurative mode of illustration, but a statement of actual fact.

There are two passages in The Outer Court to which I would like to call

THE ETERNAL LIGHT AND THE EMERALD TABLETS OF THOTH

your special attention. Here is the first: "When once a soul has passed through the gateway of the Temple, she goeth out no more." The other passage is a quotation from the Upanishads. It says, "If a man would find his soul, the first thing to do is to cease from evil ways."

Now these two passages are complementary to each other, as you will see presently. First, what does it mean "When a man enters the Temple he goeth out no more." Well, it is this: If we pledge ourselves to service and enter the Path, there can never be any withdrawal without utter destruction of mind and body. The higher forces which we contact on entering the Path cannot he played with, any more than you can play with fire. If we present ourselves to the Guardians of these powers as servants, it is against the law to release us from our pledge. Therefore the disciple used to he exhorted in olden times before taking his vow, and terrible ordeals were imposed upon him prior to his initiation.

Now turning to the other passage, "To cease from evil ways": Well, what is evil? And what are evil ways? There are many things which the man in the street would consider quite harmless, and yet to the disciple they are harmful. It is this difference that must be borne in mind. For the disciple to cease from evil ways means to refrain from every act (and thought is an act, let us well remember) which has not the absolute approval of the Higher Self. If the desire-nature and the mind have been so trained as to respond to every command of the Lord within, and if love has become the supreme Sovereign, ruling in the heart of the disciple, then may he pledge himself without fear of falling back, for then only can he be sure to have ceased from evil ways. There is a stage in the disciple's life which merits our special attention. It is the period of the great trial of his faith. At this stage the law of affinity makes itself felt. This well-known law which governs the mineral world holds good in the spiritual life of man. The affinities that bind atom to atom in the mineral world govern also the association of thoughts and ideas. If we try to cast aside the habits of a lifetime, as we generally do on entering the Path, then this law of affinity, which lies latent in our nature, suddenly rises against us and binds us to those tendencies which have grown up within us throughout the innumerable lives of the past. The disciple's task, having to face this opposition, is to fortify himself in his inner stronghold, and to exercise all the Divine patience of which he may be capable, in liberating himself by short degrees from the chains which he himself has forged. The quality most needful in this struggle is sweet patience. There may be failure to attain the ideal; usually there will be many failures, for even in the higher

THE ETERNAL LIGHT AND THE EMERALD TABLETS OF THOTH

altitudes of spiritual endeavor there cannot be uninterrupted progress. You remember it is said, "Even Great Ones have fallen from the threshold." So there is great need for endurance and persistence, and after every slip and fall the disciple must rise and take heart and, as the Gita tells us, "return to the charge again and again."

Before the soul can stand in the Masters' presence this battle must have been fought and won. We are of no use to Them until this has been done.

To wash the soul's feet in the blood of the heart means to tear out the old remembrances root and branch, not only to be able to control desire but to have none; not only to look longingly to the great ideal before us, but to be earnestly engaged in its realization. The mystery of the threshold is to be ready; to have our loins girded and our lamps burning awaiting the pleasure of the King and His command. The soul, which has fitted herself in good time, will find that love's labor has not been lost and that a glorious fruition awaits her on the very threshold of the Temple. But even while preparing for it in this life, the truly-enlightened aspirant finds that it is indeed worth while to obey the vision he has seen, and the calmness and serenity which surrounds him after every conquest are the heralds of the great peace which shall enter his heart when the sublime end has been achieved and the day is at an end. Then the laborer shall find rest and while resting prepare the ground for his future career in cycles yet to come and in worlds yet to be.

We come now to a very important point, one which cannot be sufficiently emphasized, and that is the best ways and means to be adopted by the disciple to minimize the dangers of falling back after the Path has once been entered. There are many books instructing us in this and each of them is good in its own way. The Holy Qabalah teaches us that in most cases the career of incarnate man upon earth is first expiation and then the acquisition of new experience. Now as to expiation, the lives of many millions of human beings are really nothing more than one long chain of expiation. Think of those masses of toiling, sorrowing, starving people who have never had a chance in their lifetime. What are they here for? But even iii the case of those whose lives are along more pleasant lines, misery is not absent. There are plenty of heart-breaks and sorrows, the causes of which are not always evident to the sufferers. These causes lie generally far back in their former lives upon earth, this present incarnation having for its object the expiation of ancient wrongs. In the case of disciples, this truth of expiation should never be lost sight of, for it supplies a much needed explanation of many otherwise puzzling experiences that advanced students are called upon to en-

THE ETERNAL LIGHT AND THE EMERALD TABLETS OF THOTH

dure.

Then there is the second object of incarnation, namely, the acquisition of new experience. This too applies to the disciple, for however detached from earthly things he may already be, he still may stand in need of some knowledge which can only be gained by his association with the children of men and by the observation of, and participation in, these manifold struggles and labors, incidental to earth-life. It is right here that he learns to be in the world but not of it.

Now before the soul can stand in the presence of the Masters, this ordeal of expiation and atonement must have been gone through. The blood of the heart in which the Soul's feet are to be washed is just this painful process of atoning for all the wrongs of days gone by. Thus the soul pays back the uttermost farthing, as all souls must do, and learns to identify herself with all that breathes and lives. No matter how humble and lowly a human creature may be, no matter how sinful and weak, the disciple who has learned his lessons aright knows all these creatures to be parts of the Great Divine Love to whom they are just as dear as he himself. Thus the Qabalah tells us that by learning this last lesson of identification with high and low, the disciple becomes a cooperator with those high whom we call Masters, and, under Their guidance and with their help, he continues his career, ever upward, and ever onward, until he enters the presence of the Ancient of Ancients, the merciful Teacher of Gods, angels and men.

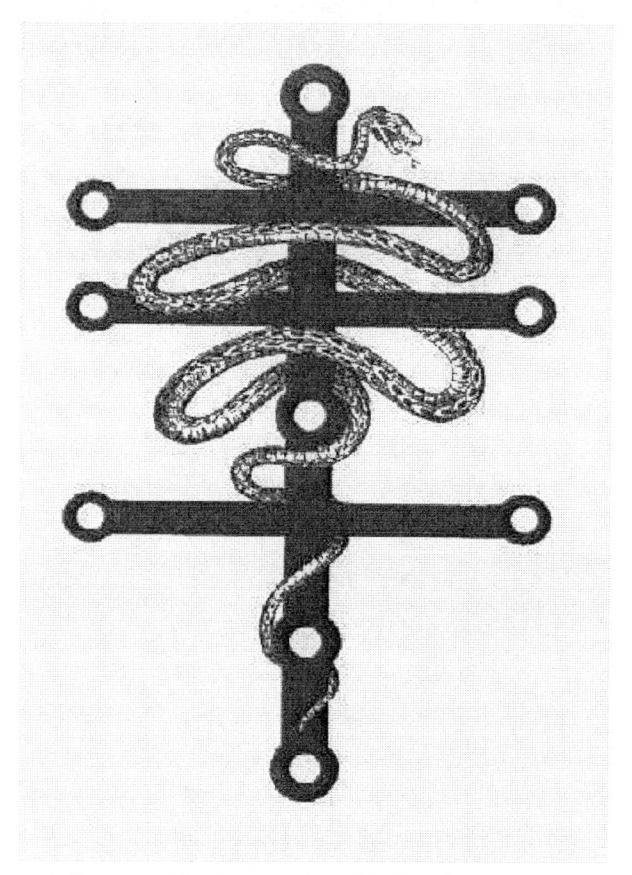

THE ETERNAL LIGHT AND THE EMERALD TABLETS OF THOTH

The Light Eternal According to the Qabalah
The secret Brotherhoods which formed the splendour of Egypt taught that life itself is the great Initiator, and the Qabalah, from which the Wisdom of the Egyptian Hierophants was derived, enjoined upon its students to "store the melody of life in their hearts" and to learn from it all that is needful.

IX.
THE LIGHT ETERNAL ACCORDING TO THE QABALAH

The Light Eternal comes from the bosom of God and shines in the eyes of every good man. It illuminates the face and lends a gentle touch to its expression and features. It is wholly absent in the countenance of the ungodly and no effort of theirs will imitate it. It is a gift from the good God to the children of light, and he bestows it upon them as a mark of his special affection.

Blessed be the man in whom this light has been lighted, for he will never lack anything needful, and even the wrath of his enemies will work goad for him. It is the light which the Prophets spoke of, and the Patriarchs desired so very much. It is the priceless pearl which it is well worth while to search after. Seek it, O Man! but not outside thee.

THE ETERNAL LIGHT AND THE EMERALD TABLETS OF THOTH

Regeneration According to the Qabalah
For what is a seed but a cylinder on which is registered in photographic script the autobiography of its evolution.

X.
REGENERATION ACCORDING TO THE QABALAH

There is a beautiful passage in the Qabalah which explains the process of regeneration in nature. I cannot quote it verbatim, but it is to the effect that whenever any substance in Nature is to be renewed and regenerated, the negative or chemical force of light assumes the reins and increases the force of repulsion within the atom so that it subdues its opponent—attraction, and the atom is repelled and separated from its neighbour atoms.

When the positive or polar forces of light again asserts its power and increases the attraction, the atom acquires new affinities, and a new substance is formed. This happens to physical-plane atoms and to spiritual-plane ones as well. The thoughtful student will grasp the analogy between the two realms of nature and understand many things suggested so forcibly by this illustration.

Is it not the same with the individual soul when the time arrives for it to renew its substance and to be regenerated? Is not the passionate, impulsive nature, the lustful flesh, wishing to do the things that grieve the Spirit, the very principle of repulsion broken loose and overbalancing the attractive power of the spiritual atom?

What a lesson for us to be kind and patient and forgiving to those in whom sin and sense are still ruling! How it teaches us to see in those who have fallen only our younger brothers and sisters in whom a natural process is going on; yea, sometimes they may he our elders upon whom nature is just putting the finishing touch. As soon as the centripetal power of attraction

THE ETERNAL LIGHT AND THE EMERALD TABLETS OF THOTH

again asserts itself in them, they may become the Helpers of their kind, Leaders and Benefactors of the race, using their experiences for the good of their unfortunate fellow-brothers and fellow-sisters.

A QABALISTIC PRAYER

Eternal God, Father of our spirit, enlighten us how to pray rightly unto thee. We would waste no vain words and we desire no material benefits. But our hearts yearn and long for the knowledge of Thee, and for Thy peace. In the fulness of Thy mercies grant us this prayer and fill our hearts with Thy love to overflowing so that we may not love only those who love us, but those who do not even know what love is. May we ever be aware of our humble origin and of our weakness in the days gone by, so that our hearts may open themselves not only to the strong who give us joy, but also to the weak ones who give us pain. It is hard for us to do it, hard indeed but enable us, O Heavenly Father, to sincerely try it and not to weary in the attempt. The road is steep, and dark is the night of our journey; our knees do often falter and we cannot as yet catch a glimpse of our eternal home, but we know that, even in the obscurity of the night, Thou art near. Unto Thee, then, we commend ourselves, and pray Thee to awaken and deepen within us the consciousness of thy presence so that we may go on our way rejoicing, until that day when our labors shall be over and we shall awaken in thy likeness.

Whatever the test that rends the soul, Whatever the grief, that floods thy sorrowing heart with tears, Whatever thy spirit fears, Let it all lift thee up, To kiss the very cross that blights thy life, For in the fulness of His grace Thou shalt see Him face to face, And after the darkness of the night Thou shalt rejoice in His glorious light.

The Emerald Tablets of Thoth The Atlantean

Explored As A Prime Source Of The Lux Aeterna

Compiled and Edited by Timothy Green Beckley
and William Kern
Published in the United States of America
by INNER LIGHT PUBLICATIONS · 2008

THE ETERNAL LIGHT AND THE EMERALD TABLETS OF THOTH

THE EMERALD TABLETS OF THOTH
by Thoth the Atlantean (Hermes Trismegistus)

TABLE OF CONTENTS
PREFACE to the original Emerald Tablets
of Thoth the Atlantean
INTRODUCTION to the original
Interpretation of the Emerald Tablets
TABLET I: The History of Thoth, The Atlantean
TABLET II: The Halls of Amenti
TABLET III: The Key of Wisdom
TABLET IV: The Space Born
TABLET V: The Dweller of Unal
TABLET VI: The Key of Magic
TABLET VII: The Seven Lords
TABLET VIII: The Key of Mysteries
TABLET IX: The Key of Freedom of Space
TABLET X: The Key of Time
TABLET XI: The Key to Above and Below
TABLET XII: The Law of Cause and Effect
and The Key of Prophecy
TABLET XIII: The Keys of Life and Death
SUPPLEMENTARY TABLET XIV
SUPPLEMENTARY TABLET XV: Secret of Secrets

THE ETERNAL LIGHT AND THE EMERALD TABLETS OF THOTH

PREFACE to the original

The history of the tablets translated in the following pages is strange and beyond the belief of modern scientists. Their antiquity is stupendous, dating back some 36,000 years B.C. The writer is Thoth, an Atlantean Priest-King, who founded a colony in ancient Egypt after the sinking of the mother country. He was the builder of the Great Pyramid of Giza, erroneously attributed to Cheops. (See The Great Pyramid by Doreal.) In it he incorporated his knowledge of the ancient wisdom and also securely secreted records and instruments of ancient Atlantis.

For some 16,000 years, he ruled the ancient race of Egypt, from approximately 50,000 B.C. to 36.000 B.C. At that time, the ancient barbarous race among which he and his followers had settled had been raised to a high degree of civilization. Thoth was an immortal, that is, he had conquered death, passing only when he willed and even then not through death. His vast wisdom made him ruler over the various Atlantean colonies, including the ones in South and Central America.

When the time came for him to leave Egypt, he erected the Great Pyramid over the entrance to the Great Halls of Amenti, placed in it his records, and appointed guards for his secrets from among the highest of his people. In later times, the descendants of these guards became the pyramid priests, by which Thoth was deified as the God of Wisdom, The Recorder, by those in the age of darkness which followed his passing. In legend, the halls of Amenti became the underworld, the Halls of the Gods, where the soul passed after death for judgment.

During later ages, the ego of Thoth passed into the bodies of men in the manner described in the tablets. As such, he incarnated three times, in his last being known as Hermes, the thrice-born. In this incarnation, he left the writings known to modern occultists as the Emerald Tablets, a later and far lesser exposition of the ancient mysteries.

THE ETERNAL LIGHT AND THE EMERALD TABLETS OF THOTH

The tablets translated in this work are ten which were left in the Great Pyramid in the custody of the pyramid priests. The ten are divided into thirteen parts for the sake of convenience. The last two are so great and far-reaching in their import that at present it is forbidden to release them to the world at large. However, in those contained herein are secrets which will prove of inestimable value to the serious student. They should be read, not once, but a hundred times for only thus can the true meaning be revealed. A casual reading will give glimpses of beauty, but more intensive study will oven avenues of wisdom to the seeker.

But now a word as to how these mighty secrets came to be revealed to modern man after being hidden so long.

Some thirteen hundred years B.C., Egypt, the ancient Khem, was in turmoil and many delegations of priests were sent to other parts of the world. Among these were some of the pyramid priests who carried with them the Emerald Tablets as a talisman by which they could exercise authority over the less advanced priest-craft of races descended from other Atlantean colonies. The tablets were understood from legend to give the bearer authority from Thoth.

The particular group of priests bearing the tablets emigrated to South America where they found a flourishing race, the Mayas who remembered much of the ancient wisdom. Among these, the priests settled and remained. In the tenth century, the Mayas had thoroughly settled the Yucatan, and the tablets were placed beneath the altar of one of the great temples of the Sun God. After the conquest of the Mayas by the Spaniards, the cities were abandoned and the treasures of the temples forgotten.

It should be understood that the Great Pyramid of Egypt has been and still is a temple of initiation into the mysteries. Jesus, Solomon, Apollonius and others were initiated there. The writer (who has a connection with the Great White Lodge which also works through the pyramid priesthood) was instructed to recover and return to the Great Pyramid the ancient tablets. This, after adventures which need not be detailed here, was accomplished. Before returning them, he was given permission to translate and retain a copy of the wisdom engraved on the tablets. This was done in 1925 and only now has permission been given for part to be published. It is expected that many will scoff. Yet the true student will read between the lines and gain wisdom. If the light is in you, the light which is engraved in these tablets will respond.

Now, a word as to the material aspect of the tablets. They consist of twelve

THE ETERNAL LIGHT AND THE EMERALD TABLETS OF THOTH

tablets of emerald green, formed from a substance created through alchemical transmutation. They are imperishable, resistant to all elements and substances. In effect, the atomic and cellular structure is fixed, no change ever taking place. In this respect, they violate the material law of ionization. Upon them are engraved characters in the ancient Atlantean language: characters which respond to attuned thought waves, releasing the associated mental vibration in the mind of the reader. The tablets are fastened together with hoops of golden-colored alloy suspended from a rod of the same material. So much for the material appearance. The wisdom contained therein is the foundation of the ancient mysteries. And for the one who reads with open eyes and mind, his wisdom shall be increased a hundred-fold.

Read. Believe or not, but read. And the vibration found therein will awaken a response in your soul.

In Cosmic Harmony,
Supreme Voice of the Brotherhood

THE ETERNAL LIGHT AND THE EMERALD TABLETS OF THOTH

INTRODUCTION to the original
An Interpretation of the Emerald Tablets

In the following pages, I will reveal some of the mysteries which as yet have only been touched upon lightly either by myself or other teachers or students of truth.

Man's search for understanding of the laws which regulate his life has been unending, yet always just beyond the veil which shields the higher planes from material man's vision the truth has existed, ready to be assimilated by those who enlarge their vision by turning inward, not outward, in their search.

In the silence of material senses lies the key to the unveiling of wisdom. He who talks does not know; he who knows does not talk. The highest knowledge is unutterable, for it exists as an entity in lanes which transcend all material words or symbols.

All symbols are but keys to doors leading to truths, and many times the door is not opened because the key seems so great that the things which are beyond it are not visible. If we can understand that all keys, all material symbols are manifestations, are but extensions of a great law and truth, we will begin to develop the vision which will enable us to penetrate beyond the veil.

All things in all universes move according to law, and the law which regulates the movement of the planets is no more immutable than the law which regulates the material expressions of man.

One of the greatest of all Cosmic Laws is that which is responsible for the formation of man as a material being. The great aim of the mystery schools of all ages has been to reveal the workings of the Law which connect man the material and man the spiritual. The connecting link between the material man and the spiritual man is the intellectual man, for the mind partakes of both the material and immaterial qualities. The aspirant for higher knowledge must develop the intellectual side of his nature and so strengthen his

THE ETERNAL LIGHT AND THE EMERALD TABLETS OF THOTH

will that is able to concentrate all powers of his being on and in the plane he desires.

The great search for light, life and love only begins on the material plane. Carried to its ultimate, its final goal is complete oneness with the universal consciousness. The foundation in the material is the first step; then comes the higher goal of spiritual attainment.

In the following pages, I will give an interpretation of the Emerald Tablets and their secret, hidden and esoteric meanings. Concealed in the words of Thoth are many meanings that do not appear on the surface. Light of knowledge brought to bear upon the Tablets will open many new fields for thought. "Read and be wise" but only if the light of your own consciousness awakens the deep-seated understanding which is an inherent quality of the soul.

In the Threefold Light

THE ETERNAL LIGHT AND THE EMERALD TABLETS OF THOTH

THE EMERALD TABLETS OF THOTH
by Thoth the Atlantean Translation by Doreal
EMERALD TABLET I:
The History of Thoth, The Atlantean

I, Thoth, the Atlantean, master of mysteries, keeper of records, mighty king, magician, living from generation to generation, being about to pass into the Halls of Amenti, set down for the guidance of those that are to come after, these records of the mighty wisdom of Great Atlantis.

In the great city of Keor on the island of Undal in a time far past, I began this incarnation. Not as the little men of the present age did the mighty ones of Atlantis live and die, but rather from aeon to aeon did they renew their life in the Halls of Amenti where the river of life flows eternally onward.

A hundred times ten have I descended the dark way that led into light, and as many times have I ascended from the darkness into the light, my strength and power renewed.

Now for a time I descend, and the men of Khem shall know me no more. But in a time yet unborn will I rise again, mighty and potent, requiring an accounting of those left behind me. Then beware, O men of Khem, if ye have falsely betrayed my teaching, for I shall cast ye down from your high estate into the darkness of the caves from whence ye came. Betray not my secrets to the men of the North or the men of the South lest my curse fall upon ye. Remember and heed my words, for surely will I return again and require of thee that which ye guard. Aye, even from beyond time and from beyond death will I return, rewarding or punishing as ye have requited your trust. Great were my people in the ancient days, great beyond the conception of the little people now around me; knowing the wisdom of old, seeking far within the heart of infinity knowledge that belonged to Earth's youth. Wise were we with the wisdom of the Children of Light who dwelt among us. Strong were we with the power drawn from the eternal fire. And of all these, great-

THE ETERNAL LIGHT AND THE EMERALD TABLETS OF THOTH

est among the children of men was my father, Thotme, keeper of the great temple, link between the Children of Light who dwelt within the temple and the races of men who inhabited the ten islands. Mouthpiece, after the three, of the Dweller of Unal, speaking to the Kings with the voice that must be obeyed.

Grew I there from a child into manhood, being taught by my father the elder mysteries, until in time there grew within the fire of wisdom, until it burst into a consuming flame. Naught desired I but the attainment of wisdom. Until on a great day the command came from the Dweller of the Temple that I be brought before him. Few there were among the children of men who had looked upon that mighty face and lived, for not as the sons of men are the Children of Light when they are not incarnate in a physical body.

Chosen was I from the sons of men, taught by the Dweller so that his purposes might be fulfilled, purposes yet unborn in the womb of time. Long ages I dwelt in the Temple, learning ever and yet ever more wisdom, until I, too, approached the light emitted from the great fire. Taught me he, the path to Amenti, the underworld where the great king sits upon his throne of might. Deep I bowed in homage before the Lords of Life and the Lords of Death, receiving as my gift the key of Life. Free was I of the Halls of Amenti, bound not by death to the circle of life. Far to the stars I journeyed until space and time became as naught. Then having drunk deep of the cup of wisdom, I looked into thehearts of men and there found I greatermysteries and was glad.For only in the Search for Truthcould my Soul be stilledand the flame within be quenched.

Down through the ages I lived, seeing those around me taste of the cup of death and return again in the light of life. Gradually from the Kingdoms of Atlantis passed waves of consciousness that had been one with me, only to be replaced by spawn of a lower star.

In obedience to the law, the word of the Master grew into flower. Downward into darkness turned the thoughts of the Atlanteans, until at last in his wrath arose from his Agwanti, the Dweller, (this word has no English equivalent; it means a state of detachment) speaking The Word, calling the power. Deep in Earth's heart, the sons of Amenti heard, and hearing, directed the changing of the flower of fire that burns eternally, changing and shifting, using the Logos, until that great fire changed its direction.

Over the world then broke the great waters, drowning and sinking, changing Earth's balance until only the Temple of Light was left standing on the great mountain on Undal still rising out of the water; some there were who

THE ETERNAL LIGHT AND THE EMERALD TABLETS OF THOTH

were living, saved from the rush of the fountains.

Called to me then the Master, saying: "Gather ye together my people. Take them by the arts ye have learned of far across the waters, until ye reach the land of the hairy barbarians, dwelling in caves of the desert. Follow there the plan that ye know of."

Gathered I then my people and entered the great ship of the Master. Upward we rose into the morning. Dark beneath us lay the Temple. Suddenly over it rose the waters. Vanished from Earth, until the time appointed, was the great Temple.

Fast we fled toward the sun of the morning, until beneath us lay the land of the children of Khem. Raging, they came with cudgels and spears lifted in anger seeking to slay and utterly destroy the Sons of Atlantis. Then raised I my staff and directed a ray of vibration, striking them still in their tracks as fragments of stone of the mountain. Then spoke I to them in words calm and peaceful, telling them of the might of Atlantis, saying we were children of the Sun and its messengers. Cowed I them by my display of magic-science, until at my feet they groveled, when I released them.

Long dwelt we in the land of Khem, long and yet long again. Until obeying the commands of the Master, who while sleeping yet lives eternally, I sent from me the Sons of Atlantis, sent them in many directions, that from the womb of time wisdom might rise again in her children.

Long time dwelt I in the land of Khem, doing great works by the wisdom within me. Upward grew into the light of knowledge the children of Khem, watered by the rains of my wisdom. Blasted I then a path to Amenti so that I might retain my powers, living from age to age a Sun of Atlantis, keeping the wisdom, preserving the records.

Great grew the sons of Khem, conquering the people around them, growing slowly upwards in Soul force. Now for a time I go from among them into the dark halls of Amenti, deep in the halls of the Earth, before the Lords of the Powers, face to face once again with the Dweller.

Raised I high over the entrance, a doorway, a gateway leading down to Amenti. Few there would be with courage to dare it, few pass the portal to dark Amenti. Raised over the passage, I, a mighty pyramid, using the power that overcomes Earth force (gravity). Deep and yet deeper placed I a force-house or chamber; from it carved I a circular passage reaching almost to the great summit. There in the apex, set I the crystal, sending the ray into the "Time-Space", drawing the force from out of the ether, concentrating upon the gateway to Amenti. (See The Great Pyramid by Doreal.)

THE ETERNAL LIGHT AND THE EMERALD TABLETS OF THOTH

Other chambers I built and left vacant to all seeming, yet hidden within them are the keys to Amenti. He who in courage would dare the dark realms, let him be purified first by long fasting. Lie in the sarcophagus of stone in my chamber. Then to reveal I to him the great mysteries. Soon shall he follow to where I shall meet him, even in the darkness of Earth shall I meet him, I, Thoth, Lord of Wisdom, meet him and hold him and dwell with him always.

Built I the Great Pyramid, patterned after the pyramid of earth force, burning eternally so that it, too, might remain through the ages. In it, I built my knowledge of "Magic-Science" so that it might be here when again I return from Amenti. Aye, while I sleep in the Halls of Amenti, my Soul roaming free will incarnate, dwell among men in this form or another. (Hermes, thrice-born.)

Emissary on Earth am I of the Dweller, fulfilling his commands so man might be lifted. Now return I to the Halls of Amenti, leaving behind me some of my wisdom. Preserve ye and keep ye the command of the Dweller: Lift ever upwards your eyes toward the light. Surely in time, ye are one with the Master, surely by right ye are one with the Master, surely by right ye are one with the All.

Now I depart from ye. Know my commandments, keep them and be them, and I will be with you, helping and guiding you into the Light.

Now before me opens the portal. Go I down in the darkness of night.

THE ETERNAL LIGHT AND THE EMERALD TABLETS OF THOTH

EMERALD TABLET II : The Halls of Amenti

Deep in the Earth's heart lie the Halls of Amenti, far 'neath the islands of sunken Atlantis, Halls of the Dead and halls of the living, bathed in the fire of the infinite ALL.

Far in a past time, lost in the space time, the Children of Light looked down on the world. See the children of men in their bondage, bound by the force that came from beyond. Knew they that only by freedom from bondage could man ever rise from the Earth to the Sun. Down they descended and created bodies, taking the semblance of men as their own. The masters of everything said after their forming: "We are they who were formed from the space-dust, partaking of life from the infinite ALL; living in the world as children of men, like and yet unlike the children of men. Then for a dwelling place, far 'neath the earth crust, blasted great spaces they by their power, spaces apart from the children of men. Surrounded them by forces and power, shielded from harm they the Halls of the Dead.

Side by side then, placed they other spaces, filled them with Life and with Light from above. Builded they then the Halls of Amenti, that they might dwell eternally there living with life to eternity's end.

Thirty and two were there of the children, sons of Light who had come among men, seeking to free from the bondage of darkness those who were bound by the force from beyond.

Deep in the Halls of Life grew a flower, flaming, expanding, driving backward the night. Placed in the center, a ray of great potence, Life giving, Light giving, filling with power all who came near it. Placed they around it thrones, two and thirty, places for each of the Children of Light, placed so that they were bathed in the radiance, filled with the Life from the eternal Light. There time after time placed they their first created bodies so that they might be filled with the Spirit of Life. One hundred years out of each thousand must the Life-giving Light flame forth on their bodies. Quickening, awakening

THE ETERNAL LIGHT AND THE EMERALD TABLETS OF THOTH

the Spirit of Life.

There in the circle from aeon to aeon, sit the Great Masters, living a life not known among men. There in the Halls of Life they lie sleeping; free flows their Soul through the bodies of men. Time after time, while their bodies lie sleeping, incarnate they in the bodies of men. Teaching and guiding onward and upward, out of the darkness into the Light. There in the Hall of Life, filled with their wisdom, known not to the races of man, living forever 'neath the cold fire of life, sit the Children of Light. Times there are when they awaken, come from the depths to be lights among men, infinite they among finite.

He who by progress has grown from the darkness, lifted himself from the night into light, free is he made of the Halls of Amenti, free of the Flower of Light and of Life. Guided he then, by wisdom and knowledge, passes from man, to the Master of Life. There he may dwell as one with the Masters, free from the bonds of the darkness of night.

Seated within the flower of radiance sit seven Lords from the Space-Time above us, helping and guiding through infinite Wisdom, the pathway through time of the children of men. Mighty and strange, they, veiled with their power, silent, all-knowing, drawing the Life force, different yet one with the children of men. Aye, different, and yet one with the Children of Light.

Custodians and watchers of the force of man's bondage, ready to loose when the light has been reached. First and most mighty, sits the Veiled Presence, Lord of Lords, the infinite Nine, over the others from each Cosmic cycle, weighing and watching the progress of men.

Under HE, sit the Lords of the Cycles; Three, Four, Five, and Six, Seven, Eight, each with his mission, each with his power, guiding, directing the destiny of man. There sit they, mighty and potent, free of all time and space. Not of this world they, yet akin to it, Elder Brothers they, of the children of men. Judging and weighing, they with their wisdom, watching the progress Light among men.

There before them was I led by the Dweller, watched him blend with ONE from above. Then from HE came forth a voice saying: "Great art thou, Thoth, among children of men. Free henceforth of the Halls of Amenti, Master of Life among children of men. Taste not of death except as thou will it, drink thou of Life to Eternity's end. Henceforth forever is Life, thine for the taking. Henceforth is Death at the call of thy hand. Dwell here or leave here when thou desireth, free is Amenti to the Sun of man. Take thou up Life in what form thou desireth, Child of the Light that has grown among men. Choose

THE ETERNAL LIGHT AND THE EMERALD TABLETS OF THOTH

thou thy work, for all souls must labor, never be free from the pathway of Light. One step thou has gained on the long pathway upward, infinite now is the mountain of Light. Each step thou taketh but heightens the mountain; all of thy progress but lengthens the goal. Approach ye ever the infinite Wisdom, ever before thee recedes the goal. Free are ye made now of the Halls of Amenti to walk hand in hand with the Lords of the world, one in one purpose, working together, bringers of Light to the children of men."

Then from his throne came one of the Masters, taking my hand and leading me onward, through all the Halls of the deep hidden land. Led he me through the Halls of Amenti, showing the mysteries that are known not to man. Through the dark passage, downward he led me into the Hall where sits the dark Death. Vast as space lay the great Hall before me, walled by darkness but yet filled with Light.

Before me arose a great throne of darkness, veiled on it seated a figure of night. Darker than darkness sat the great figure, dark with a darkness not of the night. Before it then paused the Master, speaking The Word that brings about Life, saying: "Oh, master of darkness, guide of the way from Life unto Life, before thee I bring a Sun of the morning. Touch him not ever with the power of night. Call not his flame to the darkness of night. Know him, and see him, one of our brothers, lifted from darkness into the Light. Release thou his flame from its bondage, free let it flame through the darkness of night."

Raised then the hand of the figure, forth came a flame that grew clear and bright. Rolled back swiftly the curtain of darkness, unveiled the Hall from the darkness of night. Then grew in the great space before me, flame after flame, from the veil of the night. Uncounted millions leaped they before me, some flaming forth as flowers of fire. Others there were that shed a dim radiance, glowing but faintly from out of the night. Some there were that faded swiftly; others that grew from a small spark of light. Each surrounded by its dim veil of darkness, yet flaming with the light that could never be quenched. Coming and going like fireflies in springtime, filled they the space with Light and with Life.

Then spoke a voice, mighty and solemn, saying: "These are lights that are souls among men, growing and fading, existing forever, changing yet living, through death into life. When they have bloomed into flower, reached the zenith of growth in their life, swiftly then send I my veil of darkness, shrouding and changing to new forms of life. Steadily upward throughout the ages, growing, expanding into yet greater flame, lighting the darkness

THE ETERNAL LIGHT AND THE EMERALD TABLETS OF THOTH

with yet greater power, quenched yet unquenched by the veil of the night. So grows the soul of man ever upward, quenched yet unquenched by the darkness of night.

I, Death, come, and yet I remain not, for life eternal exists in the All; only an obstacle, I in the pathway, quick to be conquered by the infinite light. Awaken, O flame that burns ever inward, flame forth and conquer the veil of the night."

Then in the midst of the flames in the darkness grew there one that drove forth the night, flaming, expanding, ever brighter, until at last was nothing but Light. Then spoke my guide, the voice of the master: "See your own soul as it grows in the light, free now forever from the Lord of the night."

Forward he led me through many great spaces filled with the mysteries of the Children of Light; mysteries that man may never yet know of until he, too, is a Sun of the Light. Backward then HE led me into the Light of the Hall of the Light. Knelt I then before the great Masters, Lords of ALL from the cycles above.

Spoke HE then with words of great power saying: "Thou has been made free of the Halls of Amenti. Choose thou thy work among the children of men."

Then spoke I: "O, great master, let me be a teacher of men, leading them onward and upward until they too, are lights among men; freed from the veil of the night that surrounds them, flaming with light that shall shine among men."

Spoke to me then the voice: "Go, as ye will. So be it decreed. Master are ye of your destiny, free to take or reject at will. Take ye the power, take ye the wisdom. Shine as a light among the children of men."

Upward then, led me the Dweller. Dwelt I again among children of men, teaching and showing some of my wisdom; Sun of the Light, a fire among men.

Now again I tread the path downward, seeking the light in the darkness of night. Hold ye and keep ye, preserve my record, guide shall it be to the children of men.

THE ETERNAL LIGHT AND THE EMERALD TABLETS OF THOTH

EMERALD TABLET III: The Key of Wisdom

I, Thoth, the Atlantean, give of my wisdom, give of my knowledge, give of my power. Freely I give to the children of men. Give that they, too, might have wisdom to shine through the world from the veil of the night. Wisdom is power and power is wisdom, one with each other, perfecting the whole.

Be thou not proud, O man, in thy wisdom. Discourse with the ignorant as well as the wise. If one comes to thee full of knowledge, listen and heed, for wisdom is all.

Keep thou not silent when evil is spoken for Truth like the sunlight shines above all.

He who over-steppeth the Law shall be punished, for only through Law comes the freedom of men.

Follow thine heart during thy lifetime. Do thou more than is commanded of thee.

When thou has gained riches, follow thou thine heart, for all these are of no avail if thine heart be weary. Diminish thou not the time of following thine heart. It is abhorred of the soul.

They that are guided go not astray, but they that are lost cannot find a straight path. If thou go among men, make for thyself, Love, the beginning and end of the heart.

If one cometh unto thee for council, let him speak freely, that the thing for which he hath come to thee may be done. If he hesitates to open his heart to thee, it is because thou, the judge, doeth the wrong.

Repeat thou not extravagant speech, neither listen thou to it, for it is the utterance of one not in equilibrium. Speak thou not of it, so that he before thee may know wisdom.

Silence is of great profit. An abundance of speech profiteth nothing.

Exalt not thine heart above the children of men, lest it be brought lower than the dust.

THE ETERNAL LIGHT AND THE EMERALD TABLETS OF THOTH

If thou be great among men, be honored for knowledge and gentleness.

If thou seeketh to know the nature of a friend, ask not his companion, but pass a time alone with him. Debate with him, testing his heart by his words and his bearing.

That which goeth into the store-house must come forth, and the things that are thine must be shared with a friend.

Knowledge is regarded by the fool as ignorance, and the things that are profitable are to him hurtful. He liveth in death. It is therefore his food.

The wise man lets his heart overflow but keeps silent his mouth.

O man, list to the voice of wisdom; list to the voice of light. Mysteries there are in the Cosmos that unveiled fill the world with their light. Let he who would be free from the bonds of darkness first divine the material from the immaterial, the fire from the earth; for know ye that as earth descends to earth, so also fire ascends unto fire and becomes one with fire. He who knows the fire that is within himself shall ascend unto the eternal fire and dwell in it eternally.

Fire, the inner fire, is the most potent of all force, for it overcometh all things and penetrates to all things of the Earth.

Man supports himself only on that which resists. So Earth must resist man else he existeth not.

All eyes do not see with the same vision, for to one an object appears of one form and color and to a different eye of another. So also the infinite fire, changing from color to color, is never the same from day to day.

Thus, speak I, Thoth, of my wisdom, for man is a fire burning bright through the night; never is quenched in the veil of the darkness, never is quenched by the veil of the night.

Hark ye, O man, and list to this wisdom: where do name and form cease? Only in consciousness, invisible, an infinite force of radiance bright. The forms that ye create by brightening thy vision are truly effects that follow thy cause.

Man is a star bound to a body, until in the end, he is freed through his strife. Only struggle and toiling thy utmost shall the star within thee bloom out in new life. He who knows the commencement of all things, free is his star from the realms of night.

Remember, O man, that all which exists is only another form of that which exists not. Everything that has being is passing into yet other being and thou thyself are not an exception.

Consider the Law, for all is Law. Seek not that which is not of the Law, for

THE ETERNAL LIGHT AND THE EMERALD TABLETS OF THOTH

such exists only in the illusions of the senses.

Wisdom cometh to all her children even as they cometh unto wisdom.

All through the ages, the light has been hidden. Awake, O man, and be wise.

Deep in the mysteries of life have I traveled, seeking and searching for that which is hidden. List ye, O man, and be wise.

Far 'neath the earth crust, in the Halls of Amenti, mysteries I saw that are hidden from men.

Oft have I journeyed the deep hidden passage, looked on the Light that is Life among men. There 'neath the Flowers of Life ever living, searched I the hearts and the secrets of men. Found I that man is but living in darkness, light of the great fire is hidden within.

Before the Lords of hidden Amenti learned I the wisdom I give unto men. Masters are they of the great Secret Wisdom, brought from the future of infinity's end. Seven are they, the Lords of Amenti, overlords they of the Children of Morning, Suns of the Cycles, Masters of Wisdom. Formed are not they as the children of men? Three, Four, Five and Six, Seven, Eight, Nine are the titles of the Masters of men.

Far from the future, formless yet forming, came they as teachers for the children of men. Live they forever, yet not of the living, bound not to life and yet free from death. Rule they forever with infinite wisdom, bound yet not bound to the dark Halls of Death. Life they have in them, yet life that is not life, free from all are the Lords of the ALL.

Forth from them came forth the Logos, instruments they of the power o'er all. Vast is their countenance, yet hidden in smallness, formed by a forming, known yet unknown.

Three holds the key of all hidden magic, creator he of the Halls of the Dead; sending forth power, shrouding with darkness, binding the souls of the children of men; sending the darkness, binding the soul force; director of negative to the children of men.

Four is he who looses the power. Lord, he, of Life to the children of men.

Light is his body, flame is his countenance; freer of souls to the children of men.

Five is the master, the Lord of all magic-Key to The Word that resounds among men.

Six is the Lord of Light, the hidden pathway, part of the souls of the children of men.

Seven is he who is Lord of the vastness, master of Space and the key of the

THE ETERNAL LIGHT AND THE EMERALD TABLETS OF THOTH

Times.

Eight is he who orders the progress; weighs and balances the journey of men.

Nine is the father, vast he of countenance, forming and changing from out of the formless.

Meditate on the symbols I give thee. Keys are they, though hidden from men.

Reach ever upward, O Soul of the morning. Turn thy thoughts upward to Light and to Life. Find in the keys of the numbers I bring thee, light on the pathway from life unto life.

Seek ye with wisdom. Turn thy thoughts inward. Close not thy mind to the Flower of Light.

Place in thy body a thought-formed picture. Think of the numbers that lead thee to Life.

Clear is the pathway to he who has wisdom. Open the door to the Kingdom of Light.

Pour forth thy flame as a Sun of the morning. Shut out the darkness and live in the day.

Take thee, O man! As part of thy being, the Seven who are but are not as they seem. Opened, O man! Have I my wisdom. Follow the path in the way I have led.

Masters of Wisdom, Sun of the Morning Light and Life to the children of men.

THE ETERNAL LIGHT AND THE EMERALD TABLETS OF THOTH

EMERALD TABLET IV: The Space Born

List ye, O man, to the voice of wisdom, list to the voice of Thoth, the Atlantean. Freely I give to thee of my wisdom gathered from the time and space of this cycle; master of mysteries, Sun of the morning, Thoth the teacher of men, is of ALL.

Long time ago, I in my childhood, lay 'neath the stars on long-buried Atlantis, dreaming of mysteries far above men. Then in my heart grew there a great longing to conquer the pathway that led to the stars. Year after year, I sought after wisdom, seeking new knowledge, following the way, until at last my Soul, in great travail, broke from its bondage and bounded away. Free was I from the bondage of earth-men. Free from the body, I flashed through the night. Unlocked at last for me was the star-space. Free was I from the bondage of night. Now to the end of space sought I wisdom, far beyond knowledge of finite man.

Far into space, my Soul traveled freely into infinity's circle of light. Strange, beyond knowledge, were some of the planets, great and gigantic, beyond dreams of men. Yet found I Law, in all of its beauty, working through and among them as here among men. Flashed forth my soul through infinity's beauty, far through space I flew with my thoughts.

Rested I there on a planet of beauty. Strains of harmony filled all the air. Shapes there were, moving in Order, great and majestic as stars in the night; mounting in harmony, ordered equilibrium, symbols of the Cosmic, like unto Law.

Many the stars I passed in my journey, many the races of men on their worlds; some reaching high as stars of the morning, some falling low in the blackness of night. Each and all of them struggling upward, gaining the heights and plumbing the depths, moving at times in realms of brightness, living through darkness, gaining the Light.

Know, O man, that Light is thine heritage. Know that darkness is only a

THE ETERNAL LIGHT AND THE EMERALD TABLETS OF THOTH

veil. Sealed in thine heart is brightness eternal, waiting the moment of freedom to conquer, waiting to rend the veil of the night.

Some I found who had conquered the ether. Free of space were they while yet they were men. Using the force that is the foundation of ALL things, far in space constructed they a planet, drawn by the force that flows through the ALL; condensing, coalescing the ether into forms that grew as they willed. Outstripping in science, they, all of the races, mighty in wisdom, sons of the stars.

Long time I paused, watching their wisdom. Saw them create from out of the ether cities gigantic of rose and gold. Formed forth from the primal element, base of all matter, the ether far flung.

Far in the past, they had conquered the ether, freed themselves from the bondage of toil; formed in their mind only a picture and swiftly created, it grew.

Forth then, my soul sped, throughout the Cosmos, seeing ever, new things and old; learning that man is truly space-born, a Sun of the Sun, a child of the stars.

Know ye, O man, whatever form ye inhabit, surely it is one with the stars. Thy bodies are nothing but planets revolving around their central suns. When ye have gained the light of all wisdom, free shall ye be to shine in the ether- one of the Suns that light outer darkness-one of the space-born grown into Light. Just as the stars in time lose their brilliance, light passing from them into the great source, so, O man, thy soul passes onward, leaving behind the darkness of night.

Formed forth ye, from the primal ether, filled with the brilliance that flows from the source, bound by the ether coalesced around, yet ever it flames until at last it is free. Lift up your flame from out of the darkness, fly from they night and ye shall be free.

Traveled I through the space-time, knowing my soul at last was set free, knowing that now might I pursue wisdom. Until at last, I passed to a plane, hidden from knowledge, known not to wisdom, extension beyond all that we know. Now, O man, when I had this knowing, happy my soul grew, for now I was free. Listen, ye space-born, list to my wisdom: know ye not that ye, too, will be free.

List ye again, O man, to my wisdom, that hearing, ye too, might live and be free. Not of the earth are ye-earthy, but child of the Infinite Cosmic Light.

Now, to ye, I give knowledge, freedom to walk in the path I have trod, showing ye truly how by my striving, I trod the path that leads to the stars.

THE ETERNAL LIGHT AND THE EMERALD TABLETS OF THOTH

Hark ye, O man, and know of thy bondage, know how to free thyself from the toils. Out of the darkness shall ye rise upward, one with the Light and one with the stars. Follow ye ever the path of wisdom. Only by this can ye rise from below. Ever man's destiny leads him onward into the Curves of Infinity's ALL.

Know ye, O man, that all space is ordered. Only by Order are ye One with the ALL. Order and balance are the Law of the Cosmos. Follow and ye shall be One with the ALL.

He who would follow the pathway of wisdom, open must be to the Flower of Life, extending his consciousness out of the darkness, flowing through time and space in the ALL.

Deep in the silence, first ye must linger until at last ye are free from desire, free from the longing to speak in the silence. Conquer by silence, the bondage of words. Abstaining from eating until ye have conquered desire for food, that is bondage of soul.

Then lie ye down in the darkness. Close ye your eyes from the rays of the Light.

Center thy soul-force in the place of thine consciousness, shaking it free from the bonds of the night. Place in thy mind-place the image thou desireth. Picture the place thou desireth to see. Vibrate back and forth with thy power. Loosen the soul from out of its night. Fiercely must thou shake with all of thy power until at last thy soul shall be free.

Mighty beyond words is the flame of the Cosmic, hanging in planes, unknown to man; mighty and balanced, moving in Order, music of harmonies, far beyond man. Speaking with music, singing with color, flame from the beginning of Eternity's ALL.

Spark of the flame art thou, O my children, burning with color and living with music. List to the voice and thou shalt be free. Consciousness free is fused with the Cosmic, One with the Order and Law of the ALL.

Knew ye not man, that out of the darkness, Light shall flame forth, a symbol of ALL.

Pray ye this prayer for attaining of wisdom. Pray for the coming of Light to the ALL. "Mighty Spirit of Light that shines through the Cosmos, draw my flame closer in harmony to thee. Lift up my fire from out of the darkness, magnet of fire that is One with the ALL. Lift up my soul, thou mighty and potent. Child of the Light, turn not away. Draw me in power to melt in thy furnace; One with all things and all things in One, fire of the life-strain and One with the Brain."

THE ETERNAL LIGHT AND THE EMERALD TABLETS OF THOTH

When ye have freed thy soul from its bondage, know that for ye the darkness is gone. Ever through space ye may seek wisdom, bound not by fetters forged in flesh.

Onward and upward into the morning, free flash, O Soul, to the realms of Light. Move thou in Order, move thou in Harmony, freely shalt move with the Children of Light.

Seek ye and know ye, my Key of Wisdom. Thus, O man, ye shall surely be free.

THE ETERNAL LIGHT AND THE EMERALD TABLETS OF THOTH

EMERALD TABLET V: The Dweller of Unal

Oft dream I of buried Atlantis, lost in the ages that have passed into night. Aeon on aeon thou existed in beauty, a shining through the darkness of night.

Mighty in power, ruling the earth-born, Lord of the Earth in Atlantis' day. King of the nations, master of wisdom, Light through Suntal, Keeper of the Way, dwelt in his Temple, the Master of Unal, Light of the Earth in Atlantis' day.

Master, He, from a cycle beyond us, living in bodies as one among men. Not as the earth-born, He from beyond us, Sun of a cycle, advanced beyond men.

Know ye, O man, that Horlet the Master, was never one with the children of men. Far in the past time when Atlantis first grew as a power, appeared there one with the Key of Wisdom, showing the way of Light to all.

Showed he to all men the path of attainment, way of the Light that flows among men. Mastering darkness, leading the Man-Soul, upward to heights that were One with the Light.

Divided the Kingdoms, He into sections. Ten were they, ruled by children of men. Upon another, built He a Temple, built but not by the children of men.

Out of the Ether called He its substance, moulded and formed by the power of Ytolan into the forms He built with His mind. Mile upon mile it covered the island, space upon space it grew in its might. Black, yet not black, but dark like the space-time, deep in its heart the Essence of Light. Swiftly the Temple grew into being, moulded an shaped by the Word of the Dweller, called from the formless into a form.

Builded He then, within it, great chambers, filled them from forms called forth from the Ether, filled them with wisdom called forth by His mind.

Formless was He within his Temple, yet was He formed in the image of man. Dwelling among them yet not of them, strange and far different was He

THE ETERNAL LIGHT AND THE EMERALD TABLETS OF THOTH

from the children of men.

Chose He then from among the people, Three who became his gateway. Chose He the Three from the Highest to become his links with Atlantis. Messengers they, who carried his councel, to the kings of the children of men.

Brought He forth others and taught them wisdom; teachers, they, to the children of men. Placed He them on the island of Undal to stand as teachers of Light to men.

Each of those who were thus chosen, taught must he be for years five and ten. Only thus could he have understanding to being Light to the children of men. Thus there came into being the Temple, a dwelling place for the Master of man.

I, Thoth, have ever sought wisdom, searching in darkness and searching in Light. Long in my youth I traveled the pathway, seeking ever new knowledge to gain. Until after much striving, one of the Three, to me brought the Light. Brought He to me the commands of the Dweller, called me from darkness into the Light. Brought He me, before the Dweller, deep in the Temple before the great Fire.

There on the great throne, beheld I, the Dweller, clothed with the Light and flashing with fire. Down I knelt before that great wisdom, feeling the Light flowing through me in waves. Heard I then the voice of the Dweller: "O darkness, come into the Light. Long have ye sought the pathway to the Light. Each soul on earth that loosens its fetters shall soon be made free from the bondage of night. Forth from the darkness have ye arisen, closer approached the Light of your goal. Here ye shall dwell as one of my children, keeper of records gathered by wisdom, instrument thou of the Light from beyond. Ready be thou made to do what is needed, perserver of wisdom though the ages of darkness that shall come fast on the children of men. Live thee here and drink of all wisdom. Secrets and mysteries unto thee shall unveil."

Then answered I, the Master of Cycles, saying: "O Light, that descended to men, give thou to me of thy wisdom that I might be a teacher of men. Give thou of thy Light that I may be free."

Spoke then to me again, the Master: "Age after age shall ye live through your wisdom. Aye, when o'er Atlantis the ocean waves roll, holding the Light, though hidden in darkness, ready to come when e'er thou shalt call. Go thee now and learn greater wisdom. Grow thou through Light to Infinity's ALL."

Long then dwelt I in the Temple of the Dweller until at last I was One with the Light.

Followed I then the path to the star planes, followed I then the pathway to

THE ETERNAL LIGHT AND THE EMERALD TABLETS OF THOTH

Light. Deep into Earth's heart I followed the pathway, learning the secrets, below as above; learning the pathway to the Halls of Amenti; learning the Law that balances the world. To earth's hidden chambers pierced I by my wisdom, deep through the Earth's crust, into the pathway, hidden for ages from the children of men. Unveiled before me, ever more wisdom until I reached a new knowledge: found that all is part of an ALL, great and yet greater than all that we know. Searched I Infinity's heart through the ages. Deep and yet deeper, more mysteries I found.

Now, as I look back through the ages, know I that wisdom is boundless, ever grown greater throughout the ages, One with Infinity's greater than all.

Light there was in ancient Atlantis. Yes, darkness, too, was hidden in all. Fell from the Light into the darkness, some who had risen to heights among men. Proud they became because of their knowledge, proud were they of their place among men. Deep delved they into the forbidden, opened the gateway that led to below. Sought they to gain ever more knowledge but seeking to bring it up from below.

He who descends below must have balance, else he is bound by lack of our Light. Opened, they then, by their knowledge, pathways forbidden to man.

But, in His Temple, all-seeing, the Dweller, lay in his Agwanti, which through Atlantis His soul roamed free. Saw He the Atlanteans, by their magic, opening the gateway that would bring to Earth a great woe. Fast fled His soul then, back to His body. Up He arose from His Agwanti. Called He the Three mighty messengers. Gave the commands that shattered the world.

Deep 'neath Earth's crust to the Halls of Amenti, swiftly descended the Dweller. Called He then on the powers of the Seven Lords wielded; changed the Earth's balance. Down sank Atlantis beneath the dark waves.

Shattered the gateway that had been opened; shattered the doorway that led down below. All of the islands were shattered except Unal, and part of the island of the sons of the Dweller. Preserved He them to be the teachers, Lights on the path for those to come after, Lights for the lesser children of man.

Called He then, I Thoth, before him, gave me commands for all I should do, saying: "Take thou, O Thoth, all of your wisdom. Take all your records. Take all your magic. Go thou forth preserving the records until in time Light grows among men. Light shalt thou be all through the ages, hidden yet found by enlightened men. Over all Earth, give WE ye power, free thou to give or

THE ETERNAL LIGHT AND THE EMERALD TABLETS OF THOTH

take it away. Gather thou now the sons of Atlantis. Take them and flee to the people of the rock caves. Fly to the land of the Children of Khem."

Then gathered I the sons of Atlantis. Into the spaceship I brought all my records, brought the records of sunken Atlantis. Gathered I all of my powers, instruments many of mighty magic.

Up then we rose on wings of the morning. High we arose above the Temple, leaving behind the three and Dweller, deep in the Halls 'neath the Temple. Down 'neath the waves sank the great Temple, closing the pathway to the Lords of the Cycles. Yet ever to him who has knowing, open shall be the path to Amenti.

Fast fled we then on the wings of the morning, fled to the land of the children of Khem. There by my power, I conquered and ruled them. Raised I to Light, the children of Khem.

Deep 'neath the rocks, I buried my spaceship, waiting the time when man might be free. Over the spaceship, erected a marker in the form of a lion yet like unto man. There 'neath the image rests yet my spaceship, forth to be brought when need shall arise.

Know ye, O man, that far in the future invaders shall come from out of the deep. Then awake, ye who have wisdom. Bring forth my ship and conquer with ease.

Deep 'neath the image lies my secret. Search and find in the pyramid I built. Each to the other is the Keystone; each the gateway that leads into Life. Follow the Key I leave behind me. Seek and the doorway to Life shall be thine. Seek thou in my pyramid, deep in the passage that ends in a wall. Use thou the Key of the Seven, and open to thee the pathway will fall.

Now unto thee I have given my wisdom. Now unto thee I have given my way. Follow the pathway. Solve thou my secrets. Unto thee I have shown the way.

THE ETERNAL LIGHT AND THE EMERALD TABLETS OF THOTH

EMERALD TABLET VI: The Key of Magic

Hark ye, O man, to the wisdom of magic. Hark to the knowledge of powers forgotten. Long, long ago in the days of the first man, warfare began between darkness and light. Men, then as now, were filled with both darkness and light; and while in some darkness held sway, in others light filled the soul.

Aye, age old is this warfare, the eternal struggle between darkness and light. Fiercely is it fought all through the ages, using strange powers hidden to man.

Adepts have there been filled with the blackness, struggling always against the light; but others there are who, filled with brightness, have ever conquered the darkness of night. Where e'er ye may be in all ages and planes, surely ye shall know of the battle with night. Long ages ago, the Suns of the Morning, descending, found the world filled with night. There in that past time began the struggle, the age old battle of darkness and Light.

Many in that time were so filled with darkness that only feebly flamed the light from the night.

Some there were, masters of darkness, who sought to fill all with their darkness; sought to draw others into their night. Fiercely withstood they, the masters of brightness; fiercely fought they from the darkness of night. Sought they ever to tighten the fetters, the chains that bind man to the darkness of night. Used they always the dark magic, brought into man by the power of darkness; magic that enshrouded man's soul with darkness.

Banded together in as order, Brothers of Darkness, they through the ages, antagonists they to the children of men. Walked they always secret and hidden, found yet not found by the children of men. Forever they walked and worked in darkness, hiding from the light in the darkness of night. Silently, secretly, use they their power, enslaving and binding the souls of men.

Unseen they come and unseen they go. Man in his ignorance calls Them

THE ETERNAL LIGHT AND THE EMERALD TABLETS OF THOTH

from below.

Dark is the way the Dark Brothers travel, dark with a darkness not of the night, traveling o'er Earth they walk through man's dreams. Power have they gained from the darkness around them to call other dwellers from out of their plane in ways that are dark and unseen by man. Into man's mind-space reach the Dark Brothers. Around it, they close the veil of their night. There through its lifetime that soul dwells in bondage, bound by the fetters of the Veil of the night. Mighty are they in the forbidden knowledge, forbidden because it is one with the night.

Hark ye, O man, and list to my warning: be ye free from the bondage of night. Surrender not your soul to the Brothers of Darkness. Keep thy face ever turned toward the Light. Know ye not, O man, that your sorrow only has come through the Veil of the night? Aye, man, heed ye my warning: strive ever upward, turn your soul toward the Light. For well know they that those who have traveled far towards the Sun on their pathway of Light have great and yet greater power to bind with darkness the children of Light.

List ye, O man, to he who comes to you. But weigh in the balance if his words be of Light. For many there are who walk in Dark Brightness and yet are not the children of Light. Easy it is to follow their pathway, easy to follow the path that they lead. But yes, O man, heed ye my warning: Light comes only to him who strives. Hard is the pathway that leads to the Wisdom, hard is the pathway that leads to the Light. Many shall ye find, the stones in your pathway; many the mountains to climb toward the Light. Yet know ye, O man, to him that o'ercometh, free will he be of the pathway of Light. Follow ye not the Dark Brothers ever. Always be ye a child of the Light. For know ye, O man, in the end Light must conquer and darkness and night be banished from Light.

Listen, O man, and heed ye this wisdom; even as darkness, so is the Light.

When darkness is banished and all Veils are rendered, out there shall flash from the darkness, the Light.

Even as exist among men the Dark Brothers, so there exists the Brothers of Light. Antagonists they of the Brothers of Darkness, seeking to free men from the night. Powers have they, mighty and potent. Knowing the Law, the planets obey. Work they ever in harmony and order, freeing the man-soul from its bondage of night. Secret and hidden, walk they also. Known not are they to the children of men. Yet know that ever they walk with thee, showing the Way to the children of men. Ever have They fought the Dark Brothers, conquered and conquering time without end. Yet always Light shall in the

THE ETERNAL LIGHT AND THE EMERALD TABLETS OF THOTH

end be master, driving away the darkness of night.

Aye, man, know ye this knowing: always beside thee walk the Children of Light.

Masters they of the Sun power, ever unseen yet the guardians of men. Open to all is their pathway, open to he who will walk in the Light. Free are They of Dark Amenti, free of the Halls where Life regins supreme. Suns are they and Lords of the morning, Children of Light to shine among men. Like man are they and yet are unlike. Never divided were they in the past. One have they been in Oneness eternal, throughout all space since the beginning of time. Up did they come in Oneness with the All One, up from the first-space, formed and unformed.

Given to man have they secrets that shall guard and protect him from all harm. He who would travel the path of a master, free must he be from the bondage of night. Conquer must he the formless and shapeless; conquer must he the phantom of fear. Knowing, must he gain of all the secrets, travel the pathway that leads through the darkness, yet ever before him keep the light of his goal. Obstacles great shall he meet in the pathway, yet press on to the Light of the Sun.

Hear ye, O man, the Sun is the symbol of the Light that shines at the end of thy road. Now to thee give I the secrets: how to meet the dark power, meet and conquer the fear from the night. Only by knowing can ye conquer; only by knowing can ye have Light.

Now I give unto thee the knowledge, known to the Masters; the knowing that conquers all the dark fears. Use this, the wisdom I give thee. Master thou shalt be of the Brothers of Night.

When unto thee there comes a feeling, drawing thee nearer to the dark gate, examine thine heart and find if the feeling thou hast has come from within. If thou shalt find the darkness thine own thoughts, banish them forth from place in thy mind. Send through thy body a wave of vibration, irregular first and regular second, repeating time after time until free. Start the Wave Force in thy Brain Center. Direct it in waves from thine head to thy foot.

But if thou findest thine heart is not darkened, be sure that a force is directed to thee. Only by knowing can thou overcome it. Only by wisdom can thou hope to be free. Knowledge brings wisdom and wisdom is power. Attain and ye shall have power o'er all.

Seek ye first a place bound with darkness. Place ye a circle around about thee. Stand erect in the midst of the circle. Use thou this formula, and thou

THE ETERNAL LIGHT AND THE EMERALD TABLETS OF THOTH

shalt be free. Raise thou thine hands to the dark space above thee. Close thou thine eyes and draw in the Light. Call to the Spirit of Light through the Space-Time, using these words and thou shalt be free: "Fill thou my body with Spirit of Light. Come from the Flower that shines through the darkness. Come from the Halls where the Seven Lords rule. Name them by name, I, the Seven: Three, Four, Five and Six, Seven, Eight-Nine. By their names I call them to aid me, free me and save me from the darkness of night: Untanas, Quertas, Chietal, and Goyana, Huertal, Semveta-Ardal. By their names I implore thee, free me from darkness and fill me with Light."

Know ye, O man, that when ye have done this, ye shall be free from the fetters that bind ye, cast off the bondage of the Brothers of Night. See ye not that the names have the power to free by vibration the fetters that bind? Use them at need to free thou thine brother so the he, too, may come forth from the night.

Thou, O man, art thy brother's helper. Let him not lie in the bondage of night.

Now unto thee, give I my magic. Take it and dwell on the pathway of Light.

Light unto thee, Life unto thee, Sun may thou be on the cycle above.

THE ETERNAL LIGHT AND THE EMERALD TABLETS OF THOTH

EMERALD TABLET VII : The Seven Lords

Hark ye, O man, and list to my Voice. Open thy mind-space and drink of my wisdom. Dark is the pathway of Life that ye travel. Many the pitfalls that lie in thy way. Seek ye ever to gain greater wisdom. Attain and it shall be light on thy way.

Open thy Soul, O man, to the Cosmic and let it flow in as one with thy Soul. Light is eternal and darkness is fleeting. Seek ye ever, O man, for the Light. Know ye that ever as Light fills thy being, darkness for thee shall soon disappear.

Open thy soul to the Brothers of Brightness. Let them enter and fill thee with Light. Lift up thine eyes to the Light of the Cosmos. Keep thou ever thy face to the goal. Only by gaining the light of all wisdom, art thou one with the Infinite goal. Seek ye ever the Oneness eternal. Seek ye ever the Light of the goal.

Light is infinite and Light is finite, separate only by darkness in man. Seek ye to rend the Veil of the Darkness. Bring thou together the Light into One.

Hear ye, O man, list to my Voice singing the song of Light and of Life. Throughout all space, Light is prevalent, encompassing ALL with its banners of flame. Seek ye forever in the Veil of the Darkness, somewhere ye shall surely find Light. Hidden and buried, lost to man's knowledge, deep in the finite the Infinite exists. Lost, but existing, flowing through all things, living in ALL is the Infinite Brain. In all space, there is only One wisdom. Though seeming divided, it is One in the One. All that exists comes forth from the Light, and the Light comes forth from the ALL.

Everything created is based upon Order: Law rules the space where the Infinite dwells. Forth from equilibrium came the great cycles, moving in harmony toward Infinity's end.

Know ye, O man, that far in the space-time, Infinity itself shall pass into change. Here ye and list to the Voice of Wisdom: Know that ALL is of ALL

THE ETERNAL LIGHT AND THE EMERALD TABLETS OF THOTH

evermore. Know that through time thou may pursue wisdom and find ever more light on the way. Aye, thou shalt find that ever receding, thy goal shall elude thee from day unto day.

Long time ago, in the Halls of Amenti, I, Thoth, stood before the Lords of the cycles. Mighty, They in their aspects of power; mighty, They in the wisdom unveiled.

Led by the Dweller, first did I see them. But afterwards free was I of their presence, free to enter their conclave at will. Oft did I journey down the dark pathway unto the Hall where the Light ever glows.

Learned I of the Masters of cycles, wisdom brought from the cycles above us, knowledge brought from Infinity's All. Many the questions I asked of the Lords of the cycles. Great was the wisdom they gave unto me. Now unto thee I give of this wisdom, drawn from the flame of Infinity's fire.

Deep in the Dark Halls sit the Seven, units of consciousness from cycles above. Manifest They in this cycle as guide of man to the knowledge of All. Seven are they, mighty in power, speaking these words through me to men. Time after time, stood I before them listening to words that came not with sound.

Once said They unto me: "O man, wouldst thou gain wisdom? Seek for it in the heart of the flame. Wouldst thou gain knowledge of power? Seek ye it in the heart of the flame. Wouldst be one with the heart of the flame? Seek then within thine own hidden flame."

Many the times spoke They to me, teaching me wisdom not of the world; showing me ever new paths to brightness; teaching me wisdom brought from above. Giving knowledge of operation, learning of Law, the order of ALL.

Spoke to me again, the Seven, saying: "From far beyond time are We come, O man. Traveled We from beyond the Space-Time, aye, from the place of Infinity's end. When ye and all of thy brethren were formless, formed forth were We from the order of ALL. Not as men are We though once We, too, were as men. Out of the Great Void were We formed forth in order and by Law. For know ye that that which is formed truly is formless, having form only to thine eyes."

And again, unto me spoke the Seven, saying: "Child of the Light, O Thoth, art thou, free to travel the bright path upward until at the last All Ones become One.

Forth were We formed after our order: Three, Four, Five and Six, Seven, Eight-Nine. Know ye that these are the number of cycles that We descend

THE ETERNAL LIGHT AND THE EMERALD TABLETS OF THOTH

from unto man. Each having here a duty to fulfill; each having here a force to control. Yet are We, One, with the Soul of our cycle. Yet are We, too, seeking a goal. Far beyond man's conception, Infinity extends into a greater than All. There, in a time that is yet not a time, we shall ALL become ONE with a greater than ALL. Time and space are moving in circles. Know ye their law, and ye, too, shall be free. Aye, free shall ye be to move through the cycles- pass the guardians that dwell at the door."

Then to me spoke He of Nine, saying: "Aeons and aeons have I existed, knowing not Life, and tasting not death. For know ye, O man, that far in the future, life and death shall be one with the All. Each so perfected by balancing the other that neither exists in the Oneness of All. In men of this cycle, the life force is rampant, but life in its growth becomes one with the All. Here, I manifest in this your cycle, but yet am I there in your future of time. Yet to me, time exists not, for in my world time exists not, for formless are We. Life have We not but yet have existence, fuller and greater and freer than thee.

Man is a flame bound to a mountain, but We in our cycle shall ever be free. Know ye, O man, that when ye have progressed into the cycles that lengthen above, life itself will pass to the darkness and only the essence of Soul shall remain."

Then to me spoke the Lord of the Eight saying: "All that ye know is but part of little. Not as yet have ye touched on the Great. Far out in space where Light reigns supreme, came I into the Light. Formed was I also but not as ye are.

Body of Light was my formless form formed. Know I not Life and know I not Death, yet master am I of all that exists. Seek ye to find the path through the barriers. Travel the road that leads to the Light."

Spoke again to me the Nine saying: "Seek ye to find the path to beyond. Not impossible is it to grow to a consciousness above. For when Two have become One and One has become the All, know ye the barrier has lifted, and ye are made free of the road. Grow thou from form to the formless. Free may thou be of the road."

Thus, through ages I listened, learning the way to the All. Now lift I my thought to the All-Thing. List ye and hear when it calls. "O Light, all pervading, One with All and All with One, flow thou to me through the channel. Enter thou so that I may be free. Make me One with the All-Soul, shining from the blackness of night. Free let me be of all space-time, free from the Veil of the night. I, a child of the Light, command: Free from the darkness to

THE ETERNAL LIGHT AND THE EMERALD TABLETS OF THOTH

be."

Formless am I to the Light-Soul, formless yet shining with Light. Know I the bonds of the darkness must shatter and fall before light.

Now give I this wisdom. Free may ye be, O man, living in light and in brightness. Turn not thy face from the Light. Thy soul dwells in realms of brightness. Ye are a child of the Light.

Turn thy thoughts inward not outward. Find thou the Light-Soul within. Know that thou are the Master. All else is brought from within. Grow thou to realms of brightness. Hold thou thy thought on the Light. Know thou are one with the Cosmos, a flame and a Child of the Light.

Now to thee give I warning: Let not thy thought turn away. Know that the brightness flows through thy body for aye. Turn not to the Dark-Brightness that comes from the Brothers of Black. But keep thine eyes ever lifted, thy soul in tune with the Light.

Take ye this wisdom and heed it. List to my Voice and obey. Follow the pathway to brightness, and thou shalt be One with the way.

THE ETERNAL LIGHT AND THE EMERALD TABLETS OF THOTH

EMERALD TABLET VIII : The Key of Mysteries

Unto thee, O man, have I given my knowledge. Unto thee have I given of Light. Hear ye now and receive my wisdom brought from space planes above and beyond.

Not as man am I for free have I become of dimensions and planes. In each, take I on a new body. In each, I change in my form. Know I now that the formless is all there is of form.

Great is the wisdom of the Seven. Mighty are they from beyond. Manifest They through their power, filled by force from beyond.

Here ye these words of wisdom. Hear ye and make them thine own. Find in them the formless. Find ye the key to beyond. Mystery is but hidden knowledge. Know and ye shall unveil. Find the deep buried wisdom and be master of darkness and Light.

Deep are the mysteries around thee, hidden the secrets of Old. Search through the Keys of my Wisdom. Surely shall ye find the way. The gateway to power is secret, but he who attains shall receive. Look to the Light! O my brother. Open and ye shall receive. Press on through the valley of darkness. Overcome the dweller of the night. Keep ever thine eyes to the Light-Plane, and thou shalt be One with the Light.

Man is in process of changing to forms that are not of this world. Grows he in time to the formless, a plane on the cycle above. Know ye, ye must become formless before ye are one with the Light.

List ye, O man, to my voice, telling of the pathways to Light, showing the way of attainment when ye shall be One with the Light. Search ye the mysteries of Earth's heart. Learn of the Law that exists, holding the stars in their balance by the force of the primordial mist. Seek ye the flame of the Earth's Life. Bathe in the glare of its flame. Follow the three-cornered pathway until thou, too, art a flame.

Speak thou in words without voice to those who dwell down below. Enter

THE ETERNAL LIGHT AND THE EMERALD TABLETS OF THOTH

the blue-litten Temple and bathe in the fire of all life.

Know, O man, thou art complex, a being of earth and of fire. Let thy flame shine out brightly. Be thou only the fire.

Wisdom is hidden in darkness. When lit by the flame of the Soul, find thou the wisdom and be Light-Born, a Sun of the Light without form. Seek thee ever more wisdom. Find it in the heart of the flame. Know that only by striving can Light pour into thy brain. Now have I spoken with wisdom. List to my Voice and obey. Tear open the Veils of the darkness. Shine a Light on the Way.

Speak I of Ancient Atlantis, speak of the days of the Kingdom of Shadows, speak of the coming of the children of shadows. Out of the great deep were they called by the wisdom of earth-men, called for the purpose of gaining great power.

Far in the past before Atlantis existed, men there were who delved into darkness, using dark magic, calling up beings from the great deep below us. Forth came they into this cycle. Formless were they of another vibration, existing unseen by the children of earth-men. Only through blood could they have formed being. Only through man could they live in the world.

In ages past were they conquered by the Masters, driven below to the place whence they came. But some there were who remained, hidden in spaces and planes unknown to man. Lived they in Atlantis as shadows, but at times they appeared among men. Aye, when the blood was offered, forth came they to dwell among men.

In the form of man moved they amongst us, but only to sight where they as are men. Serpent-headed when the glamour was lifted but appearing to man as men among men. Crept they into the Councils, taking forms that were like unto men. Slaying by their arts the chiefs of the kingdoms, taking their form and ruling o'er man. Only by magic could they be discovered. Only by sound could their faces be seen. Sought they from the kingdom of shadows to destroy man and rule in his place.

But, know ye, the Masters were mighty in magic, able to lift the Veil from the face of the serpent, able to send him back to his place. Came they to man and taught him the secret, the Word that only a man can pronounce. Swift then they lifted the Veil from the serpent and cast him forth from place among men.

Yet, beware, the serpent still liveth in a place that is open at times to the world. Unseen they walk among thee in places where the rites have been said. Again as time passes onward shall they take the semblance of men.

THE ETERNAL LIGHT AND THE EMERALD TABLETS OF THOTH

Called may they be by the master who knows the white or the black, but only the white master may control and bind them while in the flesh.

Seek not the kingdom of shadows, for evil will surely appear. For only the master of brightness shall conquer the shadow of fear.

Know ye, O my brother, that fear is an obstacle great. Be master of all in the brightness, the shadow will soon disappear. Hear ye and heed my wisdom, the voice of Light is clear. Seek not the valley of shadow, and Light only will appear.

List ye, O man, to the depth of my wisdom. Speak I of knowledge hidden from man. Far have I been on my journey though Space-Time, even to the end of the space of this cycle. Found I there the great barrier, holding man from leaving this cycle. Aye, glimpsed the Hounds of the Barrier, laying in wait for he who would pass them. In that space where time exists not, faintly I sensed the guardians of cycles. Move they only through angles. Free are they not of the curved dimensions.

Strange and terrible are the Hounds of the Barrier. Follow they consciousness to the limits of space. Think not to escape by entering your body, for follow they fast the Soul through angles. Only the circle will give ye protection, safe from the claws of the Dweller in Angles.

Once, in a time past, I approached the great Barrier, and saw on the shores where time exists not, the formless forms of the Hounds of the Barrier. Aye, hiding in the mist beyond time I found them; and They, scenting me afar off, raised themselves and gave the great bell cry that can be heard from cycle to cycle and moved through space toward my Soul.

Fled I then fast before them, back from time's unthinkable end. But ever after me pursued they, moving in strange angles not known to man. Aye, on the gray shore of Time-Space's end found I the Hounds of the Barrier, ravening for the Soul who attempts the beyond.

Fled I through circles back to my body. Fled, and fast after me they followed. Aye, after me the devourers followed, seeking through angles to devour my Soul.

Aye, know ye man, that the Soul who dares the Barrier may be held in bondage by the Hounds from beyond time, held till this cycle is all completed and left behind when the consciousness leaves.

Entered I my body. Created the circles that know not angles, created the form that from my form was formed. Made my body into a circle and lost the pursuers in the circles of time. But, even yet, when free from my body, cautious ever must I be not to move through angles, else my Soul might never

THE ETERNAL LIGHT AND THE EMERALD TABLETS OF THOTH

be free.

Know ye, the Hounds of the Barrier move only through angles and never through curves of space. Only by moving through curves can ye escape them, for in angles they will pursue thee. O man, heed ye my warning; Seek not to break open the gate to beyond. Few there are who have succeeded in passing the Barrier to the greater Light that shines beyond. For know ye, ever the dwellers, seek such Souls to hold in their thrall.

Listen, O man, and heed ye my warning; seek ye to move not in angles but curves. And if while free from thy body, thou hearest the sound like the bay of a hound ringing clear and bell-like through thy being, flee back to thy body through circles, penetrate not the mist before.

When thou hast entered the form thou hast dwelt in, use thou the cross and the circle combined. Open thy mouth and use thou thy Voice. Utter the Word and thou shalt be free. Only the one who of Light has the fullest can hope to pass by the guards of the way. And then must he move through strange curves and angles that are formed in direction not known to man.

List ye, O man, and heed ye my warning: attempt not to pass the guards in the way. Rather should ye seek to gain of thine own Light and make thyself ready to pass on the way.

Light is thine ultimate end, O my brother. Seek and find ever the Light on thy way.

THE ETERNAL LIGHT AND THE EMERALD TABLETS OF THOTH

EMERALD TABLET IX:
The Key of Freedom of Space

List ye, O man, hear ye my voice, teaching of Wisdom and Light in this cycle; teaching ye how to banish the darkness, teaching ye how to bring Light in thy life.

Seek ye, O man, to find the great pathway that leads to eternal Life as a Sun. Draw ye away from the veil of the darkness. Seek to become a Light in the world. Make of thyself a vessel for Light, a focus for the Sun of this space.

Lift thou thine eyes to the Cosmos. Lift thou thine eyes to the Light. Speak in the words of the Dweller, the chant that calls down the Light. Sing thou the song of freedom. Sing thou the song of the Soul. Create the high vibration that will make thee One with the Whole. Blend all thyself with the Cosmos. Grow into One with the Light. Be thou a channel of order, a pathway of Law to the world.

Thy Light, O man, is the great Light, shining through the shadow of flesh. Free must thou rise from the darkness before thou art One with the Light.

Shadows of darkness surround thee. Life fills thee with its flow. But know, O man, thou must arise and forth from thy body go far to the planes that surround thee and yet are One with thee, too.

Look all around thee, O man. See thine own light reflected. Aye, even in the darkness around thee, thine own Light pours forth through the veil.

Seek thou for wisdom always. Let not thine body betray. Keep in the path of the Light wave. Shun thou the darkened way. Know thee that wisdom is lasting, existing since the All-Soul began, creating harmony from chaos by the Law that exists in the Way.

List ye, O man, to the teaching of wisdom. List to the voice that speaks of the past-time. Aye, I shall tell thee knowledge forgotten, tell ye of wisdom hidden in past-time, lost in the mist of darkness around me.

Know ye, man, ye are the ultimate of all things. Only the knowledge of this

THE ETERNAL LIGHT AND THE EMERALD TABLETS OF THOTH

is forgotten, lost when man was cast into bondage, bound and fettered by the chains of the darkness.

Long, long ago, I cast off my body. Wandered I free through the vastness of ether, circled the angles that hold man in bondage. Know ye, O man, ye are only a spirit. The body is nothing. The Soul is All. Let not your body be a fetter. Cast off the darkness and travel in Light. Cast off your body, O man, and be free, truly a Light that is One with the Light.

When ye are free from the fetters of darkness and travel in space as a Sun of the Light, then ye shall know that space is not boundless but truly bounded by angles and curves. Know ye, O man, that all that exists is only an aspect of greater things yet to come. Matter is fluid and flows like a stream, constantly changing from one thing to another.

All through the ages has knowledge existed; never been changed, though buried in darkness; never been lost, though forgotten by man.

Know ye that throughout the space that ye dwell in are others as great as your own, interlaced through the heart of your matter yet separate in space of their own.

Once in a time long forgotten, I, Thoth, opened the doorway, penetrated into other spaces and learned of the secrets concealed. Deep in the essence of matter are many mysteries concealed.

Nine are the interlocked dimensions, and Nine are the cycles of space. Nine are the diffusions of consciousness, and Nine are the worlds within worlds. Aye, Nine are the Lords and the cycles that come from above and below.

Space is filled with concealed ones, for space is divided by time. Seek ye the key to the time-space, and ye shall unlock the gate. Know ye that throughout the time-space consciousness surely exists. Though from our knowledge it is hidden, yet still it forever exists.

The key to worlds within thee are found only within. For man is the gateway of mystery and the key that is One within One.

Seek ye within the circle. Use the Word I shall give. Open the gateway within thee, and sure thou, too, shalt live. Man, ye think that ye liveth, but know it is life within death. For as sure as ye are bound to your body, for you no life exists. Only the Soul is space-free, has life that is really a life. All else is only a bondage, a fetter from which to be free.

Think not that man is earth-born, though come from the earth he may be. Man is a light-born spirit. But, without knowing, he can never be free. Darkness fetters the Soul. Only the one who is seeking may ever hope to be free.

THE ETERNAL LIGHT AND THE EMERALD TABLETS OF THOTH

Shadows around thee are falling. Darkness fills all the spaces. Shine forth, O Light of the man-soul. Fill thou the darkness of space. Ye are a Sun of the Great Light. Remember and ye shall be free. Stay not thou in the shadows. Spring forth from the darkness of night. Light, let thy Soul be, O Sun-Born, filled with glory of Light, freed from the bonds of darkness, a Soul that is One with the Light.

Thou art the key to all wisdom. Within thee is all time and space. Live not in bondage to darkness. Free thou thy Light-form from night.

"Great Light that fills all the Cosmos, flow thou fully to man. Make of his body a light-torch that shall never be quenched among men."

Long in the past, sought I wisdom, knowledge not known to man. Far to the past I traveled into the space where time began. Sought I ever new knowledge to add to the wisdom I know. Yet only, I found, did the future hold the key to the wisdom I sought.

Down to the Halls of Amenti I journeyed, the greater knowledge to seek. Asked of the Lords of the Cycles, the way to the wisdom I sought. Asked the Lords this question: "Where is the source of ALL?" Answered, in tones that were mighty, the voice of the Lord of the Nine: "Free thou thy Soul from thy body and come forth with me to the Light."

Forth I came from my body, a glittering flame in the night. Stood I before the Lords, bathed in the fire of Life. Seized was I then by a force, great beyond knowledge of man. Cast was I to the Abyss through spaces unknown to man.

Saw I moulding of Order from the chaos and angles of night. Saw I the Light spring from Order and heard the voice of the Light. Saw I the flame of the Abyss, casting forth Order and Light. Saw Order spring out of chaos. Saw Light giving forth Life.

Then heard I the voice: "Hear thou and understand. The flame is the source of all things, containing all things in potentiality. The Order that sent forth light is the Word and from the Word comes Life and the existence of all." And again spoke the voice saying: "The Life in thee is the Word. Find thou the Life within thee, and have powers to use of the Word."

Long I watched the Light-flame, pouring forth from the Essence of Fire, realizing that Life is but Order and that man is one with the fire.

Back I came to my body. Stood again with the Nine, listened to the voice of the Cycles, vibrate with powers they spoke: "Know ye, O Thoth, that Life is but the Word of the Fire. The Life force ye seek before thee is but the Word in the World as a fire. Seek ye the path to the Word and powers shall surely

THE ETERNAL LIGHT AND THE EMERALD TABLETS OF THOTH

be thine."

Then asked I of the Nine: "O Lord, show me the path. Give me the path to the wisdom. Show me the way to the Word." Answered, me then, the Lord of the Nine: "Through Order, ye shall find the way. Saw ye not that the Word came from Chaos? Saw ye not that Light came from Fire? Look in thy life for disorder. Balance and order thy life. Quell all the Chaos of emotions and thou shalt have order in Life. Order brought forth from Chaos will bring thee the Word of the Source, will give thee the power of Cycles, and make of thy Soul a force that free will extend through the ages, a perfected Sun from the Source."

Listened I to the voice and deep sank the words in my heart. For ever have I sought for order that I might draw on the word. Know ye that he who attains it must ever in Order be. For use of the Word through disorder has never and can never be.

Take ye these words, O man. As part of thy life, let them be. Seek thee to conquer disorder, and One with the Word thou shalt be.

Put forth thy effort in gaining Light on the pathway of Life. Seek to be One with the Sun-State. Seek to be solely the Light. Hold thou thy thought on the Oneness of Light with the body of man. Know that all is Order from Chaos born into Light.

THE ETERNAL LIGHT AND THE EMERALD TABLETS OF THOTH

EMERALD TABLET X: The Key of Time

List ye, O man. Take of my wisdom. Learn of the deep hidden mysteries of space. Learn of the Thought that grew in the abyss, bringing Order and Harmony in space.

Know ye, O man, that all that exists has being only because of the Law. Know ye the Law and ye shall be free, never be bound by the fetters of night.

Far, through strange spaces, have I journeyed into the depth of the abyss of time, learning strange and yet stranger mysteries, until in the end all was revealed. Know ye that mystery is only mystery when it is knowledge unknown to man. When you have plumbed the heart of all mystery, knowledge and wisdom will surely be thine.

Seek ye and learn that Time is the secret whereby ye may be free of this space.

Long have I, Thoth, sought wisdom; aye, and shall seek to eternity's end for know I that ever before receding shall move the goal I seek to attain. Even the Lords of the Cycles know that not yet have They reached the goal, for with all of their wisdom, they know that Truth ever grows.

Once, in a past time, I spoke to the Dweller. Asked of the mystery of time and space. Asked him the question that surged in my being, saying: "O Master, what is time?"

Then to me spoke He, the Master: "Know ye, O Thoth, in the beginning there was void and nothingness: a timeless, spaceless, nothingness. And into the nothingness came a thought, purposeful, all-pervading, and It filled the Void. There existed no matter, only force, a movement, a vortex of vibration of the purposeful thought that filled the Void."

And I questioned the Master, saying: "Was this thought eternal?" And answered me the Dweller, saying: "In the beginning, there was eternal thought, and for thought to be eternal, time must exist. So into the all-pervading thought grew the Law of Time. Aye, time which exists through all

THE ETERNAL LIGHT AND THE EMERALD TABLETS OF THOTH

space, floating in a smooth, rhythmic movement that is eternally in a state of fixation. Time changes not, but all things change in time. For time is the force that holds events separate, each in its proper place. Time is not in motion, but ye move through time as your consciousness moves from one event to another. Aye, by time ye exist, all in all, an eternal One existence. Know ye that even though in time ye are separate, yet still are One in all times existent." Ceased then the voice of the Dweller, and departed I to ponder on time. For knew I that in these words lay wisdom and a way to explore the mysteries of time.

Oft did I ponder the words of the Dweller. Then sought I to solve the mystery of time. Found I that time moves through strange angles. Yet only by curves could I hope to attain the key that would give me access to the time-space. Found I that only by moving upward and yet again by moving to rightward could I be free from the time of this movement.

Forth I came from out of my body, moved in the movements that changed me in time. Strange were the sights I saw in my journeys, many the mysteries that opened to view. Aye, saw I man's beginning, learned from the past that nothing is new.

Seek ye, O man, to learn the pathway that leads through the spaces that are formed forth in time.

Forget not, O man, with all of thy seeking that Light is the goal ye shall seek to attain. Search ye ever for Light on thy pathway and ever for thee the goal shall endure. Let not thine heart turn ever to darkness. Light let thine Soul be, a sun on the way. Know ye that in the eternal brightness, ye shall ever find thy Soul hid in the Light, never fettered by bondage to darkness, ever it shines forth a Sun of the Light.

Aye, know, though hidden in darkness, your Soul, a spark of the true flame, exists. Be ye One with the greatest of all Lights. Find at the Source, the End of thy goal.

Light is life, for without the great Light nothing can ever exist. Know ye, that in all formed matter, the heart of Light always exists. Aye, even though bound in the darkness, inherent Light always exists.

Once I stood in the Halls of Amenti and heard the voice of the Lords of Amenti, saying in tones that rang through the silence, words of power, mighty and potent. Chanted they the song of the cycles, the words that opened the path to beyond. Aye, I saw the great path opened and looked for an instant into the beyond. Saw I the movements of the cycles, vast as the thought of the Source could convey.

THE ETERNAL LIGHT AND THE EMERALD TABLETS OF THOTH

Knew I then that even Infinity is moving on to some unthinkable end. Saw I that the Cosmos is Order and part of a movement that extends to all space, a part of an Order of Orders, constantly moving in a harmony of space. Saw I the wheeling of cycles like vast circles across the sky. Knew I then that all that has being is growing to meet yet other being in a far-off grouping of space and of time. Knew I then that in Words are power to open the planes that are hidden from man. Aye, that even in Words lies hidden the key that will open above and below.

Hark ye now, man, this word I leave with thee. Use it and ye shall find power in its sound. Say ye, the word: "Zin-Uru" and power ye shall find. Yet must ye understand that man is of Light and Light is of man.

List ye, O man, and hear a mystery stranger than all that lies 'neath the Sun. Know ye, O man, that all space is filled by worlds within worlds; aye, one within the other yet separate by Law.

Once in my search for deep buried wisdom, I opened the door that bars Them from man. Called I from other planes of being, one who was fairer than the daughters of men. Aye, I called her from out of the spaces to shine as a Light in the world of men.

Used I the drum of the Serpent. Wore I the robe of the purple and gold. Placed on my head, I, the crown of Silver. Around me the circle of cinnabar shone. Raised I my arms and cried the invocation that opens the path to the planes beyond, cried to the Lords of the Signs in their houses: "Lords of the two horizons, watchers of the treble gates, stand ye One at the right and One at the left as the Star rises to his throne and rules over his sign. Aye, thou dark prince of Arulu, open the gates of the dim, hidden land and release her whom ye keep imprisoned.

Hear ye, hear ye, hear ye, dark Lords and Shining Ones, and by their secret names, names which I know and can pronounce, hear ye and obey my will."

Lit I then with flame my circle and called Her in the space-planes beyond. "Daughter of Light return from Arulu. Seven times and seven times have I passed through the fire. Food have I not eaten. Water have I not drunk. I call thee from Arulu, from the realm of Ekershegal, I summon thee, Lady of Light."

Then before me rose the dark figures; aye, the figures of the Lords of Arulu. Parted they before me and forth came the Lady of Light. Free was she now from the Lords of the night, free to live in the Light of the earth Sun, free to live as a child of Light.

Here ye and listen, O my children. Magic is knowledge and only is Law.

THE ETERNAL LIGHT AND THE EMERALD TABLETS OF THOTH

Be not afraid of the power within thee for it follows Law as the stars in the sky.

Know ye that to he without knowledge, wisdom is magic and not of the Law. But know ye that ever ye by your knowledge can approach closer to a place in the Sun.

List ye, my children, follow my teaching. Be ye ever seeker of Light. Shine in the world of men all around thee, a Light on the path that shall shine among men.

Follow ye and learn of my magic. Know that all force is thine if thou wilt. Fear not the path that leads thee to knowledge, but rather shun ye the dark road.

Light is thine, O man, for the taking. Cast off the fetters and thou shalt be free. Know ye that thy Soul is living in bondage fettered by fear that holds ye in thrall. Open thy eyes and see the great Sun-Light. Be not afraid for all is thine own. Fear is the Lord of dark Arulu to he who has never faced the dark fear. Aye, know that fear has existence created by those who are bound by their fears.

Shake off thy bondage, O children, and walk in the Light of the glorious day. Never turn thy thoughts to the darkness and surely ye shall be One with the Light.

Man is only what he believeth, a brother of darkness or a child of the Light. Come thou into the Light my Children. Walk in the pathway that leads to the Sun.

Hark ye now and list to the wisdom. Use thou the word I have given unto thee. Use it and surely thou shalt find power and wisdom and Light to walk in the way. Seek thee and find the key I have given and ever shalt thou be a Child of the Light.

THE ETERNAL LIGHT AND THE EMERALD TABLETS OF THOTH

EMERALD TABLET XI:
The Key to Above and Below

Hear ye and list ye, O children of Khem, to the words that I give that shall bring ye to the Light. Ye know, O men, that I knew your fathers, aye, your fathers in a time long ago. Deathless have I been through all the ages, living among ye since your knowledge began. Leading ye upward to the Light of the Great Soul have I ever striven, drawing ye from out of the darkness of night.

Know ye, O people amongst whom I walk, that I, Thoth, have all of the knowledge and all of the wisdom known to man since the ancient days. Keeper have I been of the secrets of the great race, holder of the key that leads into life. Bringer up have I been to ye, O my children, even from the darkness of the Ancient of Days. List ye now to the words of my wisdom. List ye now to the message I bring. Hear ye now the words I give thee, and ye shall be raised from the darkness to Light.

Far in the past, when first I came to thee, found I thee in caves of rocks. Lifted I thee by my power and wisdom until thou didst shine as men among men. Aye, found I thee without any knowing. Only a little were ye raised beyond beasts. Fanned I ever the spark of thy consciousness until at last ye flamed as men.

Now shall I speak to thee knowledge ancient beyond the thought of thy race. Know ye that we of the Great Race had and have knowledge that is more than man's. Wisdom we gained from the star-born races, wisdom and knowledge far beyond man's. Down to us had descended the masters of wisdom as far beyond us as I am from thee. List ye now while I give ye wisdom. Use it and free thou shalt be.

Know ye that in the pyramid I builded are the Keys that shall show ye the Way into life. Aye, draw ye a line from the great image I builded, to the apex of the pyramid, built as a gateway. Draw ye another opposite in the same

THE ETERNAL LIGHT AND THE EMERALD TABLETS OF THOTH

angle and direction. Dig ye and find that which I have hidden. There shall ye find the underground entrance to the secrets hidden before ye were men.

Tell ye I now of the mystery of cycles that move in movements that are strange to the finite, for infinite are they beyond knowledge of man. Know ye that there are nine of the cycles; aye, nine above and fourteen below, moving in harmony to the place of joining that shall exist in the future of time. Know ye that the Lords of the Cycles are units of consciousness sent from the others to unify This with the All. Highest are They of the consciousness of all the Cycles, working in harmony with the Law. Know They that in time all will be perfected, having none above and none below, but all One in a perfected Infinity, a harmony of all in the Oneness of All.

Deep 'neath Earth's surface in the Halls of Amenti sit the Seven, the Lords of the Cycles, aye, and another, the Lord from below. Yet know thee that in Infinity there is neither above nor below. But ever there is and ever shall be Oneness of All when all is complete. Oft have I stood before the Lords of the All. Oft at the fount of their wisdom have drunken and filled both my body and Soul with their Light.

Spake they to me and told me of cycles and the Law that gives them the means to exist. Aye, spake to me the Lord of the Nine saying: "O, Thoth, great are ye among Earth's children, but mysteries exist of which ye know not. Ye know that ye came from a space-time below this and know ye shall travel to a space-time beyond. But little ye know of the mysteries within them, little ye know of the wisdom beyond. Know ye that ye as a whole in this consciousness are only a cell in the process of growth.

The consciousness below thee is ever-expanding in different ways from those known to thee. Aye, it, though in space-time below thee, is ever growing in ways that are different from those that were part of the ways of thine own. For know that it grows as a result of thy growth but not in the same way that thou didst grow. The growth that thou had and have in the present have brought into being a cause and effect. No consciousness follows the path of those before it, else all would be repetition and vain. Each consciousness in the cycle it exists in follows its own path to the ultimate goal. Each plays its part in the Plan of the Cosmos. Each plays its part in the ultimate end. The farther the cycle, the greater its knowledge and ability to blend the Law of the whole.

Know ye, that ye in the cycles below us are working the minor parts of the Law, while we of the cycle that extends to Infinity take of the striving and build greater Law.

THE ETERNAL LIGHT AND THE EMERALD TABLETS OF THOTH

Each has his own part to play in the cycles. Each has his work to complete in his way. The cycle below thee is yet not below thee but only formed for a need that exists. For know ye that the fountain of wisdom that sends forth the cycles is eternally seeking new powers to gain. Ye know that knowledge is gained only by practice, and wisdom comes forth only from knowledge, and thus are the cycles created by Law. Means are they for the gaining of knowledge for the Plane of Law that is the Source of the All. The cycle below is not truly below but only different in space and in time. The consciousness there is working and testing lesser things than those ye are. And know, just as ye are working on greater, so above ye are those who are also working as ye are on yet other laws. The difference that exists between the cycles is only in ability to work with the Law. We, who have being in cycles beyond thee, are those who first came forth from the Source and have in the passage through time-space gained ability to use Laws of the Greater that are far beyond the conception of man. Nothing there is that is really below thee but only a different operation of Law.

Look thee above or look thee below, the same shall ye find. For all is but part of the Oneness that is at the Source of the Law. The consciousness below thee is part thine own as we are a part of thine.

Ye, as a child had not the knowledge that came to ye when ye became a man. Compare ye the cycles to man in his journey from birth unto death, and see in the cycle below thee the child with the knowledge he has; and see ye yourself as the child grown older, advancing in knowledge as time passes on. See ye, We, also, the child grown to manhood with the knowledge and wisdom that came with the years. So also, O Thoth, are the cycles of consciousness, children in different stages of growth, yet all from the one Source, the Wisdom, and all to the Wisdom returning again."

Ceased then He from speaking and sat in the silence that comes to the Lords. Then again spake He unto me, saying: "O Thoth, long have We sat in Amenti, guarding the flame of life in the Halls. Yet know, we are still part of our Cycles with our Vision reaching unto them and beyond. Aye, know we that of all, nothing else matters excepting the growth we can gain with our Soul. Know we the flesh is fleeting. The things men count great are nothing to us. The things we seek are not of the body but are only the perfected state of the Soul. When ye as men can learn that nothing but progress of Soul can count in the end, then truly ye are free from all bondage, free to work in a harmony of Law.

Know, O man, ye should aim at perfection, for only thus can ye attain to

THE ETERNAL LIGHT AND THE EMERALD TABLETS OF THOTH

the goal. Though ye should know that nothing is perfect, yet it should be thy aim and thy goal." Ceased again the voice of the Nine, and into my consciousness the words had sunk. Now, seek I ever more wisdom that I may be perfect in Law with the All.

Soon go I down to the Halls of Amenti to live 'neath the cold flower of life. Ye whom I have taught shall nevermore see me. Yet live I forever in the wisdom I taught.

All that man is is because of his wisdom. All that he shall be is the result of his cause.

List ye, now to my voice and become greater than common man. Lift thine eyes upward, let Light fill thy being, be thou ever Children of Light. Only by effort shall ye grow upward to the plane where Light is the All of the All. Be ye the master of all that surrounds thee. Never be mastered by the effects of thy life. Create then ever more perfect causes and in time shalt thou be a Sun of the Light.

Free, let thine soul soar ever upward, free from the bondage and fetters of night. Lift thine eyes to the Sun in the sky-space. For thee, let it be a symbol of life. Know that thou art the Greater Light, perfect in thine own sphere, when thou art free. Look not ever into the blackness. Lift up thine eyes to the space above. Free let thine Light flame upward and shalt thou be a Child of the Light.

THE ETERNAL LIGHT AND THE EMERALD TABLETS OF THOTH

EMERALD TABLET XII: The Seven Lords

Hark ye, O man, and list to my Voice. Open thy mind-space and drink of my wisdom. Dark is the pathway of Life that ye travel. Many the pitfalls that lie in thy way. Seek ye ever to gain greater wisdom. Attain and it shall be light on thy way.

Open thy Soul, O man, to the Cosmic and let it flow in as one with thy Soul. Light is eternal and darkness is fleeting. Seek ye ever, O man, for the Light. Know ye that ever as Light fills thy being, darkness for thee shall soon disappear.

Open thy soul to the Brothers of Brightness. Let them enter and fill thee with Light. Lift up thine eyes to the Light of the Cosmos. Keep thou ever thy face to the goal. Only by gaining the light of all wisdom, art thou one with the Infinite goal. Seek ye ever the Oneness eternal. Seek ye ever the Light of the goal.

Light is infinite and Light is finite, separate only by darkness in man. Seek ye to rend the Veil of the Darkness. Bring thou together the Light into One.

Hear ye, O man, list to my Voice singing the song of Light and of Life. Throughout all space, Light is prevalent, encompassing ALL with its banners of flame. Seek ye forever in the Veil of the Darkness, somewhere ye shall surely find Light. Hidden and buried, lost to man's knowledge, deep in the finite the Infinite exists. Lost, but existing, flowing through all things, living in ALL is the Infinite Brain. In all space, there is only One wisdom. Though seeming divided, it is One in the One. All that exists comes forth from the Light, and the Light comes forth from the ALL.

Everything created is based upon Order: Law rules the space where the Infinite dwells. Forth from equilibrium came the great cycles, moving in harmony toward Infinity's end.

Know ye, O man, that far in the space-time, Infinity itself shall pass into change. Here ye and list to the Voice of Wisdom: Know that ALL is of ALL

THE ETERNAL LIGHT AND THE EMERALD TABLETS OF THOTH

evermore. Know that through time thou may pursue wisdom and find ever more light on the way. Aye, thou shalt find that ever receding, thy goal shall elude thee from day unto day.

Long time ago, in the Halls of Amenti, I, Thoth, stood before the Lords of the cycles. Mighty, They in their aspects of power; mighty, They in the wisdom unveiled.

Led by the Dweller, first did I see them. But afterwards free was I of their presence, free to enter their conclave at will. Oft did I journey down the dark pathway unto the Hall where the Light ever glows.

Learned I of the Masters of cycles, wisdom brought from the cycles above us, knowledge brought from Infinity's All. Many the questions I asked of the Lords of the cycles. Great was the wisdom they gave unto me. Now unto thee I give of this wisdom, drawn from the flame of Infinity's fire.

Deep in the Dark Halls sit the Seven, units of consciousness from cycles above. Manifest They in this cycle as guide of man to the knowledge of All. Seven are they, mighty in power, speaking these words through me to men. Time after time, stood I before them listening to words that came not with sound.

Once said They unto me: "O man, wouldst thou gain wisdom? Seek for it in the heart of the flame. Wouldst thou gain knowledge of power? Seek ye it in the heart of the flame. Wouldst be one with the heart of the flame? Seek then within thine own hidden flame."

Many the times spoke They to me, teaching me wisdom not of the world; showing me ever new paths to brightness; teaching me wisdom brought from above. Giving knowledge of operation, learning of Law, the order of ALL.

Spoke to me again, the Seven, saying: "From far beyond time are We come, O man. Traveled We from beyond the Space-Time, aye, from the place of Infinity's end. When ye and all of thy brethren were formless, formed forth were We from the order of ALL. Not as men are We though once We, too, were as men. Out of the Great Void were We formed forth in order and by Law. For know ye that that which is formed truly is formless, having form only to thine eyes."

And again, unto me spoke the Seven, saying: "Child of the Light, O Thoth, art thou, free to travel the bright path upward until at the last All Ones become One.

Forth were We formed after our order: Three, Four, Five and Six, Seven, Eight-Nine. Know ye that these are the number of cycles that We descend

THE ETERNAL LIGHT AND THE EMERALD TABLETS OF THOTH

from unto man. Each having here a duty to fulfill; each having here a force to control. Yet are We, One, with the Soul of our cycle. Yet are We, too, seeking a goal. Far beyond man's conception, Infinity extends into a greater than All. There, in a time that is yet not a time, we shall ALL become ONE with a greater than ALL. Time and space are moving in circles. Know ye their law, and ye, too, shall be free. Aye, free shall ye be to move through the cycles- pass the guardians that dwell at the door."

Then to me spoke He of Nine, saying: "Aeons and aeons have I existed, knowing not Life, and tasting not death. For know ye, O man, that far in the future, life and death shall be one with the All. Each so perfected by balancing the other that neither exists in the Oneness of All. In men of this cycle, the life force is rampant, but life in its growth becomes one with the All. Here, I manifest in this your cycle, but yet am I there in your future of time. Yet to me, time exists not, for in my world time exists not, for formless are We. Life have We not but yet have existence, fuller and greater and freer than thee.

Man is a flame bound to a mountain, but We in our cycle shall ever be free. Know ye, O man, that when ye have progressed into the cycles that lengthen above, life itself will pass to the darkness and only the essence of Soul shall remain."

Then to me spoke the Lord of the Eight saying: "All that ye know is but part of little. Not as yet have ye touched on the Great. Far out in space where Light reigns supreme, came I into the Light. Formed was I also but not as ye are.

Body of Light was my formless form formed. Know I not Life and know I not Death, yet master am I of all that exists. Seek ye to find the path through the barriers. Travel the road that leads to the Light."

Spoke again to me the Nine saying: "Seek ye to find the path to beyond. Not impossible is it to grow to a consciousness above. For when Two have become One and One has become the All, know ye the barrier has lifted, and ye are made free of the road. Grow thou from form to the formless. Free may thou be of the road."

Thus, through ages I listened, learning the way to the All. Now lift I my thought to the All-Thing. List ye and hear when it calls. "O Light, all pervading, One with All and All with One, flow thou to me through the channel. Enter thou so that I may be free. Make me One with the All-Soul, shining from the blackness of night. Free let me be of all space-time, free from the Veil of the night. I, a child of the Light, command: Free from the darkness to

THE ETERNAL LIGHT AND THE EMERALD TABLETS OF THOTH

be."

Formless am I to the Light-Soul, formless yet shining with Light. Know I the bonds of the darkness must shatter and fall before light.

Now give I this wisdom. Free may ye be, O man, living in light and in brightness. Turn not thy face from the Light. Thy soul dwells in realms of brightness. Ye are a child of the Light.

Turn thy thoughts inward not outward. Find thou the Light-Soul within. Know that thou are the Master. All else is brought from within. Grow thou to realms of brightness. Hold thou thy thought on the Light. Know thou are one with the Cosmos, a flame and a Child of the Light.

Now to thee give I warning: Let not thy thought turn away. Know that the brightness flows through thy body for aye. Turn not to the Dark-Brightness that comes from the Brothers of Black. But keep thine eyes ever lifted, thy soul in tune with the Light.

Take ye this wisdom and heed it. List to my Voice and obey. Follow the pathway to brightness, and thou shalt be One with the way.

THE ETERNAL LIGHT AND THE EMERALD TABLETS OF THOTH

EMERALD TABLET XIII:
The Keys of Life and Death

List ye, O man, hear ye the wisdom. Hear ye the Word that shall fill thee with Life. Hear ye the Word that shall banish the darkness. Hear ye the voice that shall banish the night.

Mystery and wisdom have I brought to my children; knowledge and power descended from old. Know ye not that all shall be opened when ye shall find the oneness of all? One shall ye be with the Masters of Mystery, Conquerors of Death and Masters of Life. Aye, ye shall learn of the flower of Amenti the blossom of life that shines in the Halls. In Spirit shall ye reach that Halls of Amenti and bring back the wisdom that liveth in Light. Know ye the gateway to power is secret. Know ye the gateway to life is through death. Aye, through death but not as ye know death, but a death that is life and is fire and is Light.

Desireth thou to know the deep, hidden secret? Look in thy heart where the knowledge is bound. Know that in thee the secret is hidden, the source of all life and the source of all death.

List ye, O man, while I tell the secret, reveal unto thee the secret of old.

Deep in Earth's heart lies the flower, the source of the Spirit that binds all in its form. For know ye that the Earth is living in body as thou art alive in thine own formed form. The Flower of Life is as thine own place of Spirit and streams through the Earth as thine flows through thy form; giving of life to the Earth and its children, renewing the Spirit from form unto form. This is the Spirit that is form of thy body, shaping and moulding into its form.

Know ye, O man, that thy form is dual, balanced in polarity while formed in its form. Know that when fast on thee Death approaches, it is only because thy balance is shaken. It is only because one pole has been lost.

Know that thy body when in perfect balance may never be touched by the finger of Death. Aye, even accident may only approach when the balance is gone. When ye are in a balanced equilibrium, ye shall live on in time and

THE ETERNAL LIGHT AND THE EMERALD TABLETS OF THOTH

not taste of Death. Know that thou art the balanced completion, existing because of thy balance of poles. As, in thee, one pole is drawn downward, fast from thee goes the balance of life. Then unto thee cold Death approaches, and change must come to thine unbalanced life.

Know that the secret of life in Amenti is the secret of restoring the balance of poles. All that exists has form and is living because of the Spirit of life in its poles.

See ye not that in Earth's heart is the balance of all things that exist and have being on its face? The source of thy Spirit is drawn from Earth's heart, for in thy form thou are one with the Earth.

When thou hast learned to hold thine own balance, then shalt thou draw on the balance of Earth. Exist then shalt thou while Earth is existing, changing in form, only when Earth, too, shalt change: Tasting not of death, but one with this planet, holding thy form till all pass away.

List ye, O man, whilst I give the secret so that ye, too, shalt taste not of change. One hour each day shalt thou lie with thine head pointed to the place of the positive pole (north). One hour each day shalt thy head be pointed to the place of the negative pole (south). Whilst thy head is placed to the northward, hold thou thy consciousness from the chest to the head. And when thy head is placed southward, hold thou thy thought from chest to the feet. Hold thou in balance once in each seven, and thy balance will retain the whole of its strength. Aye, if thou be old, thy body will freshen and thy strength will become as a youth's. This is the secret known to the Masters by which they hold off the fingers of Death. Neglect not to follow the path I have shown, for when thou hast passed beyond years to a hundred to neglect it will mean the coming of Death.

Hear ye, my words, and follow the pathway. Keep thou thy balance and live on in life.

Hear ye, O man, and list to my voice. List to the wisdom that gives thee of Death. When at the end of thy work appointed, thou may desire to pass from this life, pass to the plane where the Suns of the Morning live and have being as Children of Light. Pass without pain and pass without sorrow into the plane where is eternal Light.

First lie at rest with thine head to the eastward. Fold thou thy hands at the Source of thy life (solar plexus). Place thou thy consciousness in the life seat. Whirl it and divide to north and to south. Send thou the one out toward the northward. Send thou the other out to the south. Relax thou thy hold upon thy being. Forth from they form will thy silver spark fly, upward and onward

THE ETERNAL LIGHT AND THE EMERALD TABLETS OF THOTH

to the Sun of the morning, blending with Light, at one with its source. There it shall flame till desire shall be created. Then shall return to a place in a form. Know ye, O men, that thus pass the great Souls, changing at will from life unto life. Thus ever passes the Avatar, willing his Death as he wills his own life.

List ye, O man, drink of my wisdom. Learn ye the secret that is Master of Time. Learn ye how those ye call Masters are able to remember the lives of the past. Great is the secret yet easy to master, giving to thee the mastery of time. When upon thee death fast approaches, fear not but know ye are master of Death. Relax thy body, resist not with tension. Place in thy heart the flame of thy Soul. Swiftly then sweep it to the seat of the triangle. Hold for a moment, then move to the goal. This, thy goal, is the place between thine eyebrows, the place where the memory of life must hold sway. Hold thou thy flame here in thy brain-seat until the fingers of Death grasp thy Soul. Then as thou pass through the state of transition, surely the memories of life shall pass, too. Then shalt the past be as one with the present. Then shall the memory of all be retained. Free shalt thou be from all retrogression. The things of the past shall live in today.

Man, ye have heard the voice of my wisdom. Follow and ye shall live through the ages as I.

List ye, O man, hear ye the wisdom. Hear ye the Word that shall fill thee with Life. Hear ye the Word that shall banish the darkness. Hear ye the voice that shall banish the night.

Mystery and wisdom have I brought to my children; knowledge and power descended from old. Know ye not that all shall be opened when ye shall find the oneness of all? One shall ye be with the Masters of Mystery, Conquerors of Death and Masters of Life. Aye, ye shall learn of the flower of Amenti the blossom of life that shines in the Halls. In Spirit shall ye reach that Halls of Amenti and bring back the wisdom that liveth in Light. Know ye the gateway to power is secret. Know ye the gateway to life is through death. Aye, through death but not as ye know death, but a death that is life and is fire and is Light.

Desireth thou to know the deep, hidden secret? Look in thy heart where the knowledge is bound. Know that in thee the secret is hidden, the source of all life and the source of all death.

List ye, O man, while I tell the secret, reveal unto thee the secret of old.

Deep in Earth's heart lies the flower, the source of the Spirit that binds all in its form. For know ye that the Earth is living in body as thou art alive in thine own formed form. The Flower of Life is as thine own place of Spirit and

THE ETERNAL LIGHT AND THE EMERALD TABLETS OF THOTH

streams through the Earth as thine flows through thy form; giving of life to the Earth and its children, renewing the Spirit from form unto form. This is the Spirit that is form of thy body, shaping and moulding into its form.

Know ye, O man, that thy form is dual, balanced in polarity while formed in its form. Know that when fast on thee Death approaches, it is only because thy balance is shaken. It is only because one pole has been lost.

Know that thy body when in perfect balance may never be touched by the finger of Death. Aye, even accident may only approach when the balance is gone. When ye are in a balanced equilibrium, ye shall live on in time and not taste of Death. Know that thou art the balanced completion, existing because of thy balance of poles. As, in thee, one pole is drawn downward, fast from thee goes the balance of life. Then unto thee cold Death approaches, and change must come to thine unbalanced life.

Know that the secret of life in Amenti is the secret of restoring the balance of poles. All that exists has form and is living because of the Spirit of life in its poles.

See ye not that in Earth's heart is the balance of all things that exist and have being on its face? The source of thy Spirit is drawn from Earth's heart, for in thy form thou are one with the Earth.

When thou hast learned to hold thine own balance, then shalt thou draw on the balance of Earth. Exist then shalt thou while Earth is existing, changing in form, only when Earth, too, shalt change: Tasting not of death, but one with this planet, holding thy form till all pass away.

List ye, O man, whilst I give the secret so that ye, too, shalt taste not of change. One hour each day shalt thou lie with thine head pointed to the place of the positive pole (north). One hour each day shalt thy head be pointed to the place of the negative pole (south). Whilst thy head is placed to the northward, hold thou thy consciousness from the chest to the head. And when thy head is placed southward, hold thou thy thought from chest to the feet. Hold thou in balance once in each seven, and thy balance will retain the whole of its strength. Aye, if thou be old, thy body will freshen and thy strength will become as a youth's. This is the secret known to the Masters by which they hold off the fingers of Death. Neglect not to follow the path I have shown, for when thou hast passed beyond years to a hundred to neglect it will mean the coming of Death.

Hear ye, my words, and follow the pathway. Keep thou thy balance and live on in life.

Hear ye, O man, and list to my voice. List to the wisdom that gives thee of

THE ETERNAL LIGHT AND THE EMERALD TABLETS OF THOTH

Death. When at the end of thy work appointed, thou may desire to pass from this life, pass to the plane where the Suns of the Morning live and have being as Children of Light. Pass without pain and pass without sorrow into the plane where is eternal Light.

First lie at rest with thine head to the eastward. Fold thou thy hands at the Source of thy life (solar plexus). Place thou thy consciousness in the life seat. Whirl it and divide to north and to south. Send thou the one out toward the northward. Send thou the other out to the south. Relax thou thy hold upon thy being. Forth from they form will thy silver spark fly, upward and onward to the Sun of the morning, blending with Light, at one with its source. There it shall flame till desire shall be created. Then shall return to a place in a form. Know ye, O men, that thus pass the great Souls, changing at will from life unto life. Thus ever passes the Avatar, willing his Death as he wills his own life.

List ye, O man, drink of my wisdom. Learn ye the secret that is Master of Time. Learn ye how those ye call Masters are able to remember the lives of the past. Great is the secret yet easy to master, giving to thee the mastery of time. When upon thee death fast approaches, fear not but know ye are master of Death. Relax thy body, resist not with tension. Place in thy heart the flame of thy Soul. Swiftly then sweep it to the seat of the triangle. Hold for a moment, then move to the goal. This, thy goal, is the place between thine eyebrows, the place where the memory of life must hold sway. Hold thou thy flame here in thy brain-seat until the fingers of Death grasp thy Soul. Then as thou pass through the state of transition, surely the memories of life shall pass, too. Then shalt the past be as one with the present. Then shall the memory of all be retained. Free shalt thou be from all retrogression. The things of the past shall live in today.

Man, ye have heard the voice of my wisdom. Follow and ye shall live through the ages as I.

THE ETERNAL LIGHT AND THE EMERALD TABLETS OF THOTH

EMERALD TABLET XIV: Supplementary

List ye, O Man, to the deep hidden wisdom, lost to the world since the time of the Dwellers, lost and forgotten by men of this age.

Know ye this Earth is but a portal, guarded by powers unknown to man. Yet, the Dark Lords hide the entrance that leads to the Heaven-born land. Know ye, the way to the sphere of Arulu is guarded by barriers opened only to Light-born man.

Upon Earth, I am the holder of the keys to the gates of the Sacred Land. Command I, by the powers beyond me, to leave the keys to the world of man. Before I depart, I give ye the Secrets of how ye may rise from the bondage of darkness, cast off the fetters of flesh that have bound ye, rise from the darkness into the Light. Know ye, the soul must be cleansed of its darkness, ere ye may enter the portals of Light. Thus, I established among ye the Mysteries so that the Secrets may always be found. Aye, though man may fall into darkness, always the Light will shine as a guide. Hidden in darkness, veiled in symbols, always the way to the portal will be found. Man in the future will deny the mysteries but always the way the seeker will find.

Now I command ye to maintain my secrets, giving only to those ye have tested, so that the pure may not be corrupted, so that the power of Truth may prevail. List ye now to the unveiling of Mystery. List to the symbols of Mystery I give. Make of it a religion for only thus will its essence remain.

Regions there are two between this life and the Great One, traveled by the Souls who depart from this Earth; Duat, the home of the powers of illusion; Sekhet Hetspet, the House of the Gods. Osiris, the symbol of the guard of the portal, who turns back the souls of unworthy men. Beyond lies the sphere of the heaven-born powers, Arulu, the land where the Great Ones have passed. There, when my work among men has been finished, will I join the Great Ones of my Ancient home.

Seven are the mansions of the house of the Mighty; Three guards the por-

THE ETERNAL LIGHT AND THE EMERALD TABLETS OF THOTH

tal of each house from the darkness; Fifteen the ways that lead to Duat. Twelve are the houses of the Lords of Illusion, facing four ways, each of them different. Forty and Two are the great powers, judging the Dead who seek for the portal. Four are the Sons of Horus, Two are the Guards of East and West-Isis, the mother who pleads for her children, Queen of the moon, reflecting the Sun. Ba is the essence, living forever. Ka is the Shadow that man knows as life. Ba cometh not until Ka is incarnate. These are mysteries to preserve through the ages. Keys are they of life and of Death. Hear ye now the mystery of mysteries: learn of the circle beginningless and endless, the form of He who is One and in all. Listen and hear it, go forth and apply it, thus will ye travel the way that I go. Mystery in Mystery, yet clear to the Light-born, the Secret of all I now will reveal. I will declare a secret to the initiated, but let the door be wholly shut against the profane.

Three is the mystery, come from the great one. Hear, and Light on thee will dawn.

In the primeval, dwell three unities. Other than these, none can exist. These are the equilibrium, source of creation: one God, one Truth, one point of freedom.

Three come forth from the three of the balance: all life, all good, all power.

Three are the qualities of God in his Light-home: Infinite power, Infinite Wisdom, Infinite Love.

Three are the powers given to the Masters: To transmute evil, assist good, use discrimination.

Three are the things inevitable for God to perform: Manifest power, wisdom and love.

Three are the powers creating all things: Divine Love possessed of perfect knowledge, Divine Wisdom knowing all possible means, Divine Power possessed by the joint will of Divine Love and Wisdom.

Three are the circles (states) of existence: The circle of Light where dwells nothing but God, and only God can traverse it; the circle of Chaos where all things by nature arise from death; the Circle of awareness where all things spring from life.

All things animate are of three states of existence: chaos or death, liberty in humanity and felicity of Heaven.

Three necessities control all things: beginning in the Great Deep, the circle of chaos, plenitude in Heaven.

Three are the paths of the Soul: Man, Liberty, Light.

Three are the hindrances: lack of endeavor to obtain knowledge; non-

THE ETERNAL LIGHT AND THE EMERALD TABLETS OF THOTH

attachment to god; attachment to evil. In man, the three are manifest. Three are the Kings of power within. Three are the chambers of the mysteries, found yet not found in the body of man.

Hear ye now of he who is liberated, freed from the bondage of life into Light. Knowing the source of all worlds shall be open. Aye, even the Gates of Arulu shall not be barred. Yet heed, O man, who wouldst enter heaven. If ye be not worthy, better it be to fall into the fire. Know ye the celestials pass through the pure flame. At every revolution of the heavens, they bathe in the fountains of Light.

List ye, O man, to this mystery: Long in the past before ye were man-born, I dwelled in Ancient Atlantis. There in the Temple, I drank of the Wisdom, poured as a fountain of Light from the Dweller. Give the key to ascend to the Presence of Light in the Great world. Stood I before the Holy One enthroned in the flower of fire. Veiled was he by the lightnings of darkness, else my Soul by the Glory have been shattered.

Forth from the feet of his Throne like the diamond, rolled forth four rivers of flame from his footstool, rolled through the channels of clouds to the Man-world. Filled was the hall with Spirits of Heaven. Wonder of wonders was the Starry palace. Above the sky, like a rainbow of Fire and Sunlight, were formed the spirits. Sang they the glories of the Holy One. Then from the midst of the Fire came a voice: "Behold the Glory of the first Cause." I beheld that Light, high above all darkness, reflected in my own being. I attained, as it were, to the God of all Gods, the Spirit-Sun, the Sovereign of the Sun spheres.

Again came the Voice: "There is one, even the First, who hath no beginning, who hath no end; who hath made all things, who govern all, who is good, who is just, who illumines, who sustains."

Then from the throne, there poured a great radiance, surrounding and lifting my soul by its power. Swiftly I moved through the spaces of Heaven, shown was I the mystery of mysteries, shown the Secret heart of the cosmos. Carried was I to the land of Arulu, stood before the Lords in their Houses. Opened they the Doorway so I might glimpse the primeval chaos. Shuddered my soul to the vision of horror, shrank back my soul from the ocean of darkness. Then saw I the need for the barriers, saw the need for the Lords of Arulu. Only they with their Infinite balance could stand in the way of the inpouring chaos. Only they could guard God's creation.

Then did I pass 'round the circle of eight. Saw all the souls who had conquered the darkness. Saw the splendor of Light where they dwelled.

THE ETERNAL LIGHT AND THE EMERALD TABLETS OF THOTH

Longed I to take my place in their circle, but longed I also for the way I had chosen, when I stood in the Halls of Amenti and made my choice to the work I would do.

Passed I from the Halls of Arulu down to the earth space where my body lay. Arose I from the earth where I rested. Stood I before the Dweller. Gave my pledge to renounce my Great right until my work on Earth was completed, until the Age of darkness be past.

List ye, O man, to the words I shall give ye. In them shall ye find the Essence of Life. Before I return to the Halls of Amenti, taught shall ye be the Secrets of Secrets, how ye, too, may arise to the Light. Preserve them and guard them, hide them in symbols, so the profane will laugh and renounce. In every land, form ye the mysteries. Make the way hard for the seeker to tread. Thus will the weak and the wavering be rejected. Thus will the secrets be hidden and guarded, held till the time when the wheel shall be turned. Through the dark ages, waiting and watching, my Spirit shall remain in the deep hidden land. When one has passed all the trials of the outer, summon ye me by the Key that ye hold. Then will I, the Initiator, answer, come from the Halls of the Gods in Amenti. Then will I receive the initiate, give him the words of power.

Hark ye, remember, these words of warning: bring not to me one lacking in wisdom, impure in heart or weak in his purpose. Else I will withdraw from ye your power to summon me from the place of my sleeping.

Go forth and conquer the element of darkness. Exalt in thy nature thine essence of Light.

Now go ye forth and summon thy brothers so that I may impart the wisdom to light thy path when my presence is gone. Come to the chamber beneath my temple. Eat not food until three days are past. There will I give thee the essence of wisdom so that with power ye may shine amongst men. There will I give unto thee the secrets so that ye, to , may rise to the Heavens-God-men in Truth as in essence ye be. Depart now and leave me while I summon those ye know of but as yet know not.

THE ETERNAL LIGHT AND THE EMERALD TABLETS OF THOTH

EMERALD TABLET XV:
Supplementary Secret of Secrets

Now ye assemble, my children, waiting to hear the Secret of Secrets which shall give ye power to unfold the God-man, give ye the way to Eternal life. Plainly shall I speak of the Unveiled Mysteries. No dark sayings shall I give unto thee. Open thine ears now, my children. Hear and obey the words that I give.

First I shall speak of the fetters of darkness which bind ye in chains to the sphere of the Earth.

Darkness and light are both of one nature, different only in seeming, for each arose from the source of all. Darkness is disorder. Light is Order. Darkness transmuted is light of the Light. This, my children, your purpose in being; transmutation of darkness to light.

Hear ye now of the mystery of nature, the relations of life to the Earth where it dwells. Know ye, ye are threefold in nature, physical, astral and mental in one. Three are the qualities of each of the natures; nine in all, as above, so below.

In the physical are these channels, the blood which moves in vortical motion, reacting on the heart to continue its beating. Magnetism which moves through the nerve paths, carrier of energies to all cells and tissues. Akasa which flows through channels, subtle yet physical, completing the channels. Each of the three attuned with each other, each affecting the life of the body. Form they the skeletal framework through which the subtle ether flows. In their mastery lies the Secret of Life in the body. Relinquished only by will of the adept, when his purpose in living is done.

Three are the natures of the Astral, mediator is between above and below; not of the physical, not of the Spiritual, but able to move above and below.

Three are the natures of Mind, carrier it of the Will of the Great One. Arbi-

THE ETERNAL LIGHT AND THE EMERALD TABLETS OF THOTH

trator of Cause and Effect in thy life. Thus is formed the threefold being, directed from above by the power of four. Above and beyond man's threefold nature lies the realm of the Spiritual Self. Four is it in qualities, shining in each of the planes of existence, but thirteen in one, the mystical number. Based on the qualities of man are the Brothers: each shall direct the unfoldment of being, each shall channels be of the Great One.

On Earth, man is in bondage, bound by space and time to the earth plane. Encircling each planet, a wave of vibration, binds him to his plane of unfoldment. Yet within man is the Key to releasement, within man may freedom be found.

When ye have released the self from the body, rise to the outermost bounds of your earth-plane. Speak ye the word Dor-E-Lil-La. Then for a time your Light will be lifted, free may ye pass the barriers of space. For a time of half of the sun (six hours), free may ye pass the barriers of earth-plane, see and know those who are beyond thee. Yea, to the highest worlds may ye pass. See your own possible heights of unfoldment, know all earthly futures of Soul.

Bound are ye in your body, but by the power ye may be free. This is the Secret whereby bondage shall be replaced by freedom for thee.

Calm let thy mind be. At rest be thy body: Conscious only of freedom from flesh. Center thy being on the goal of thy longing. Think over and over that thou wouldst be free. Think of this word-La-Um-I-L-Gan-over and over in thy mind let it sound. Drift with the sound to the place of thy longing. Free from the bondage of flesh by thy will.

Hear ye while I give the greatest of secrets: how ye may enter the Halls of Amenti, enter the place of the immortals as I did, stand before the Lords in their places.

Lie ye down in rest of thy body. Calm thy mind so no thought disturbs thee. Pure must ye be in mind and in purpose, else only failure will come unto thee. Vision Amenti as I have told in my Tablets. Long with fullness of heart to be there. Stand before the Lords in thy mind's eye. Pronounce the words of power I give (mentally); Mekut-El-Shab-El Hale-Sur-Ben-El-Zabrut Zin-Efrim-Quar-El. Relax thy mind and thy body. Then be sure your soul will be called.

Now give I the Key to Shamballa, the place where my Brothers live in the darkness: Darkness but filled with Light of the Sun-Darkness of Earth, but Light of the Spirit, guides for ye when my day is done.

Leave thou thy body as I have taught thee. Pass to the barriers of the deep,

THE ETERNAL LIGHT AND THE EMERALD TABLETS OF THOTH

hidden place. Stand before the gates and their guardians. Command thy entrance by these words: "I am the Light. In me is no darkness. Free am I of the bondage of night. Open thou the way of the Twelve and the One, so I may pass to the realm of wisdom." When they refuse thee, as surely they will, command them to open by these words of power: "I am the Light. For me are no barriers. Open, I command, by the Secret of Secrets-Edom-El-Ahim-Sabbert-Zur Adom." Then if thy words have been "Truth" of the highest, open for thee the barriers will fall.

Now, I leave thee, my children. Down, yet up, to the Halls shall I go. Win ye the way to me, my children. Truly my brothers shall ye become.

Thus finish I my writings. Keys let them be to those who come after. But only to those who seek my wisdom, for only for these am I the Key and the Way.

DRAGONSTAR'S MENTAL MAGICK VIDEOS

Trained In An Ancient Secret Lodge With Its Lineage In Atlantis and MU the Living Avatar Brings the Art of Spellcasting Into the 21st Century

Three New DVDs That Command The Mystical and Secret Powers of the Universe

Each DVD in this series contains subliminal magickal commands that charge your super-conscious with magickal vibrations, capable of making a reality of your heart's desires. By watching these DVDs, you become an active participant in their magickal evoking energies and are able to apply them to matters needing metaphysical solutions. For best results, watch the DVD right before bed when your mind is relaxed and open to the suggestive commands in the videos.

OWN ONE OR ALL THREE IN THE CURRENT DRAGONSTAR MENTAL MAGICK SERIES

❑ **RITUALS AND SPELLS TO ATTRACT A LOVER OR SOUL MATE**—If you're looking for love and romance this DVD has magickal commands to either attract new love or enhance a current relationship. If you feel your Soul Mate is out there somewhere it will attract him or her like nothing else. Passion can be yours, but be warned – this is potent stuff.

❑ **WIN BIG! GAIN PROSPERITY! OBTAIN 'BIG MONEY' NOW!** —Fill that piggy bank to over flowing. Let the good times roll. Want a house? New car? Run a business of your own? Win the lottery? Get your money for "nothing" and your kicks for free.

❑ **ATTRACT GOOD LUCK – BANISH BAD LUCK TODAY!** —Don't roll over and play dead. Take advantage of your God given right to be lucky in all you do. No need to be cursed when negativity can be tossed right out the window (and you don't even have to open it, brother). Watching this DVD will enhance your personal vibrations, help free you from bad thoughts, and allow the good luck energies of the universe to flow through you.

Remember the Universe operates on the premise of laws of attraction. We attract to ourselves what we think, feel and project. By using the DragonStar Mental Magick DVDs, the subliminal messages allow your subconscious to free itself of the negative thoughts and feelings imposed by the conscious mind.

HOW TO ORDER—Each DVD is just $15.00. Or order all three for just $39.95. And please add $5.00 shipping and handling.

OTHER DRAGONSTAR ITEMS OF IMPORTANCE

❑ **DRAGONSTAR LIFE STUDY COURSE**—12 monthly lessons in awakening your psychic ability and becoming a master of all that is. Earn a degree in Metaphysics or Parapsychology once you have passed this home study class. **$100.00**

❑ **DEVELOP YOUR LATENT PANORMAL POWERS**—Use a magick mirror. See through solid objects. Read Minds. Dematerialize. Read the Akashic Records. Peer into the future. Fabulous workbook just **$20.00**

❑ **NEW MAGICK HANDBOOK** – Dozens of simple spells for a complex universe. **$17.50**

❑ **HOW TO TRAVEL TO OTHER DIMENSIONS** – There are many dimensions and astral planes to conquer. Find out how to get there and what you will find. Completely safe! - **$15.00**

SUPER SPECIAL — Be sure to add shipping and handling. All items this page just $175.00 + $10.00 S/H

Credit Cards 732 602-3407 · NJ residents add sales tax. Overseas double shipping fees

**Inner Light · Box 753
New Brunswick, NJ 08903
PayPal to: MrUFO8@hotmail.com**

FREE Study Course and 70 Minute CD On Understanding The Kabbalah

EXPERIENCE A VAST CHANGE IN YOUR LIFE IN JUST 14 DAYS WHEN YOU WEAR THIS

All Riches And Desires Will Come Within Easy Reach

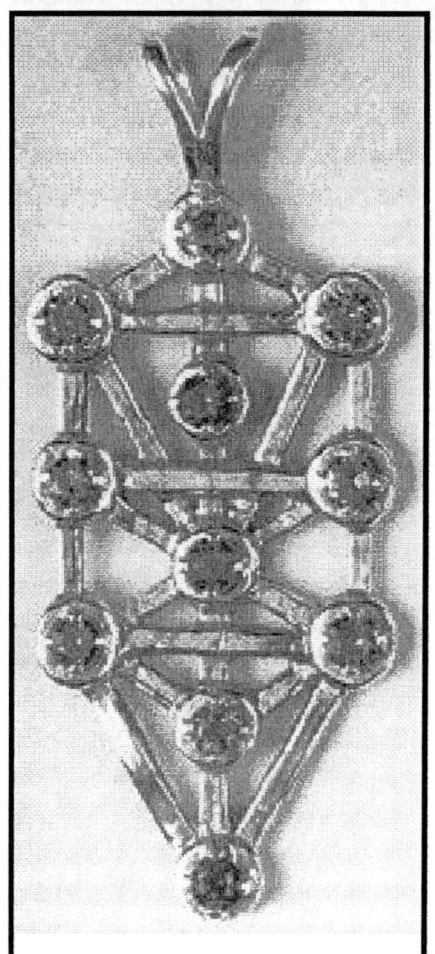

The Kabbalah has been in the news recently as numerous celebrities...such as Madonna...have begun to study and apply its ancient laws, as they go about searching for spiritual guidance in their own lives.

The non-initiated have long been taught that the Kabbalah is virtually impossible to understand and impractical to use; that is, unless a person is well educated in the ancient Biblical languages from which these sacred writings have been taken. Until now only a few learned Rabbi have retained this mystic and highly occult knowledge and they have, for the most part, kept these arcane secrets to themselves. Now, however, there are some who feel strongly, due to the need to reawaken spiritual values in the world, that this knowledge must be shared.

Among the secrets of the Kabbalah are those pertaining to the Mystical Tree Of Life. The Tree Of Life is a powerful symbol and tool for using God's energies everyday. The symbol dates from the dawn of creation and was supposed to be shared with humankind so that all good things could become manifest and we could have everything we desire in life. When used properly in prayer and meditation it, in effect, acts as a communications device to speak directly with God...a sort of Telephone To The Heavens. It is said that there is no stronger, no more powerful, amulet in all of creation.

In our research we have found a very talented jewelry crafter who has managed to capture the Tree Of Life amulet in its true Kabbalistic form. There are other, less powerful versions being sold. Individually cast in silver with 10 faceted stones, this beautiful pendant consists of two main pillars, a middle pillar, and ten spheres, or sephirot, located on each of the pillars. The spheres act as emanations or forms of energy with specific qualities and their placement is important, as the thirty-two paths that lead from one to another become paths of knowledge, awareness, wisdom and ultimately lead to oneness with God. The Tree Of Life pendant offers a deep reflection into the eternal mysteries of the universe and should only be used for beneficial and positive purposes.

Tree Of Life Pendant
These beautiful pendants are cast individually and may vary slightly from the sample shown.

A Kabbalistic Symbol with the mystic Universal Ouroboros

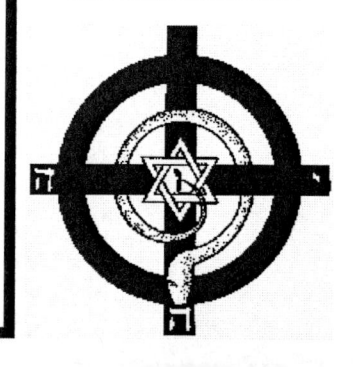

USE YOUR TREE OF LIFE PENDANT DAILY

Our Tree Of Life Magical Jeweled Pendant comes with a detailed study course consisting of a 70-minute CD, *Beginner's Guide to the Kabbalah,* to help you unlock its many secrets, as well as a Study Guide/Workbook organized by the famed avatar, DragonStar. With this course and the Tree Of Life pendant you can attract all you want in life as well as become closer to the Creator. Learn the 32 Paths of Wisdom; How to Merge With The Divine; The Ten Emanations Of The Divine; as well as how to decode specific secrets of the Universe.

❏ ALL FOR THE AMAZING LOW PRICE OF $99.95 + $5.00 S/H

TREE OF LIFE PENDANT

Old Testament Prophets Knew Its Significance

As You Proceed To Tap Its Amazing God Given Powers! **Its Power Is Still Unmatched Today!**

THE TEN BASIC BELIEFS OF KABBALAH

1. There exists an Infinite Being that is the source of everything.
2. Everything exists as a vehicle for humankind to fulfill its purpose; animate and inanimate creations are all here to serve humankind.
3. Humankind's purpose is to become one with the Creator. That is why we are here. That is what we are supposed to be doing. It is the soul's desire.
4. The way to become one with the Infinite Being is to struggle to be moral and spiritual while manifest as flesh, amidst a sea of temptations and challenges. Every situation in life is a spiritual challenge for many reasons.
5. All of humankind is interwoven and interdependent in a spiritual sense. We are all one. To become one with the Creator, one must care about humanity.
6. All that is manifest exists within the individual. Humans are microcosms of all creation. This is part of being created in the "image of the divine."
7. There is a physical realm where we exist, and there is a spiritual realm with which we unknowingly interact constantly. Every molecule manifest into our reality has a spiritual counterpart with which it is connected.
8. Our problems and challenges are actually responses from the spiritual realm, based upon our thoughts, speech, and actions, and are specifically designed for our spiritual growth.
9. History is moving toward a predetermined destiny. The Infinite Being designed our time of struggle to end by a certain period date, which will conclude our test.
10. A place has been designated that allows humankind to experience the Infinite Being. That is where those fulfilling their purpose will translocate after death of the physical body. Each person will experience the Infinite Being in a way and to the extent that person became one with the Creator while manifest as flesh on Earth.

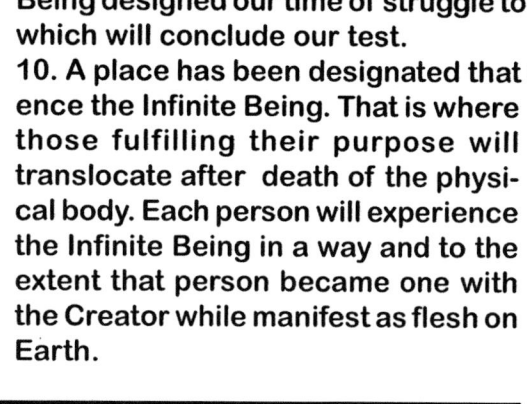

INNER LIGHT • Box 753 • New Brunswick, NJ 08903

I can't wait to show off my beautiful Tree Of Life Pendant and am enclosing $99.95 plus $5.00 for shipping and handling for this highly charged amulet of God, as well as my FREE 70-minute CD and Study Guide by DragonStar on the secrets of the Kabbalah.

NAME: _____

ADDRESS: _____

CITY/STATE/ZIP: _____

VISA, MasterCard and Discover card customers call our 24 hour secure hotline 732-602-3407 or supply card number, expiration date and signature when ordering by mail. We also accept USA bank checks, International and postal money orders. NO CASH. New Jersey residents add sales tax. All foreign please add US $15 for additional postage and insurance. Please allow adequate time for processing and delivery of your order.

Pathways To Enlightenment from the Kabbalah. Details are included in the literature you will receive.

EARN A DEGREE IN METAPHYSICS OR PARAPSYCHOLOGY

DragonStar's LIFE STUDY COURSE

❏ Check Desired Items

The Mystic Lodge of DragonStar is an ancient secret lodge with its lineage in Atlantis and MU. Now the presnt day head of the lodge, DragonStar, has been instructed to pass the teachings of the lodge on to a limited number of new students who wish to master the science of metaphysics.

The teachings of the **Mystic Lodge of DragonStar** are given in the form of a monthly home study course. Each month the enrolled student will receive a series of instructions and a questionnaire to be completed and returned to the lodge for grading. At the end of the 12-month course all graduating students will receive a Degree in Metaphysics and a proclamation entitling them to instruct others in the ways of the mystic arts.

The DragonStar Life Study Course will include in-depth study of:
- Reawakening Your Psychic Abilities
- Preparing for Spiritual Awakening
- Becoming Receptive to the Universe
- The Mystic Power of Words
- The Use of Magic Oil and Incense
- Developing Hidden Powers From Within
- Contacting the Ascended Masters For Counseling and Guidance
- Learning to Read the Past, Present and Future.

The **complete 12-month course is $100.00** and is payable in advance.

YOUR PERSONAL DRAGONSTAR DESTINY READING AND SPELL KIT ❏ ONE TIME ONLY FEE $75.00

Each day, DragonStar devotes a part of his practice to assisting those who are in trouble and in spiritual need. DragonStar teaches that we are the masters of our destinies, but that sometimes we may need the "expert" guidance of the enlightened in order to reaffirm our own private position in the cosmos. For a limited time, DragonStar will provide you with a personal **DESTINY READING** as well as a spell kit to be used in conjunction with your forecast and reading. Please provide your birth information (date, time, place) and ask two questions in your own handwriting so that he may work with your personal vibrations.

DragonStar's Spiritual Alchemy Book Library

❏ **NEW MAGICK HANDBOOK-SIMPLE SPELLS FOR A COMPLEX WORLD**—Studying the mystical arts need not be complex. Here are easy to do spells without the heavy "arcane language." Spells to Encourage Love, Affection and Romance; Increase Your Income; Improve Sexual Performance; Rid Yourself of Unwanted Relationships; Become Highly Successful In Business; Win In All Personal And Legal Matters; Rid The Physical Body of Emotional and Physical Pain—**$17.50 + $5.00 S/H**

❏ **HOW TO TRAVEL TO OTHER DIMENSIONS**— Paves the way to enter dimensions and travel freely on the various layers that have been identified by mystics for centuries as the seven planes of the astral world. Learn where the other dimensions are located; how to get there...and back; identify the good entities from the bad.—**$15.00 + $5.00 S/H**

❏ **DEVELOP YOUR LATENT PARANORMAL POWERS**—This book teaches you how to pick up a crystal ball and see into the future. Learn how to use a magic mirror. See through solid objects. Feel the thoughts of others. Learn to read minds. Eleven mini-lessons in one!—**$20.00 + $5.00 S/H**

❏ **CANDLE MAGICK DIVINATION: GOOD LUCK, GOOD FORTUNE**—Secrets of candle burning revealed. YOU can learn to mark a candle for spiritual use, locate lost objects, use the pendulum, read dice, follow the flights of birds, open your channel to higher vibrations—**$15.00 + $5.00 S/H**

❏ **ENTIRE LIBRARY—$59.95 + $5.00 S/H**

INNER LIGHT • Box 753 • New Brunswick, NJ 08903
VISA, MasterCard, Discover card customers call our 24 hour secure hotline 732-602-3407.
PayPal to MrUFO8@hotmail.com